CULTURES OF THE WORLD

PAPUA NEW GUINEA

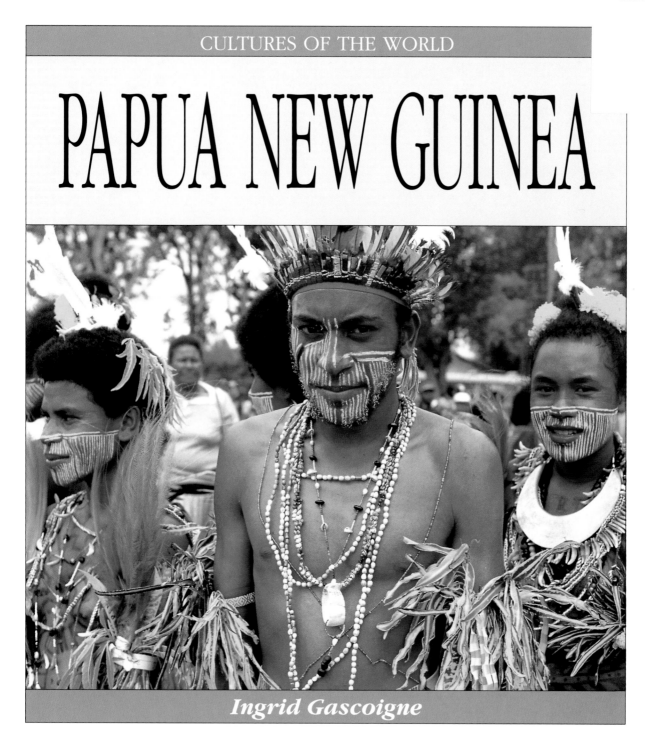

Ingrid Gascoigne

MARSHALL CAVENDISH
New York • London • Sydney

Reference edition published 1999 by
Marshall Cavendish Corporation
99 White Plains Road
Tarrytown
New York 10591

© Times Editions Pte Ltd 1998

Originated and designed by
Times Books International, an imprint of
Times Editions Pte Ltd

Printed by Times Offset Malaysia

Library of Congress Cataloging-in-Publication Data:

Gascoigne, Ingrid.
 Papua New Guinea / Ingrid Gascoigne.
  p. cm.—(Cultures of the World)
 Includes bibliographical references and index.
 Summary: Discusses the geography, history, economy,
government, varied culture and peoples of the country made
up of more than 600 islands and archipelagos.
 ISBN 0-7614-0813-4 (library binding)
 1. Papua New Guinea—Juvenile literature. [1. Papua
New Guinea.] I. Title. II. Series.
DU740.G36 1998
995.3—dc21   97–43611
              CIP
              AC

INTRODUCTION

PAPUA NEW GUINEA IS a young nation, having achieved its independence only in 1975, yet it is filled with ancient cultures that are still fused into the rhythm of daily living. This fledgling nation includes over 600 small islands and archipelagos, and its population is made up of over 700 different linguistic and ethnic groups scattered throughout its islands, living on a diverse terrain of jagged mountains, plains, fertile valleys, and swampland. The country did not enter written history until as recently as 1526, and an entire Stone Age civilization flourished in the heart of its highlands undetected by the Western world until the 1930s. It takes more than a book of this size to describe such a country in all its detail, but *Cultures of the World: Papua New Guinea* gives a comprehensive overview of a nation of hundreds of vital ancient cultures as it hurtles headlong into the 21st century.

CONTENTS

Boy eating sago, a staple food item.

CONTENTS

An animal and a human figure together make up this totem pole which belongs to a clan in Papua New Guinea.

GEOGRAPHY

PAPUA NEW GUINEA CONSISTS OF OVER 600 SMALL ISLANDS and archipelagos, along with the "mainland," the eastern section of the large island known as New Guinea. Situated just south of the equator, it lies to the north of Australia, at the edge of the Pacific Ocean. The Torres Strait, the narrowest point between mainland Australia and Papua New Guinea, is about 100 miles (160 km) across, and one of the Australian-owned Torres Islands lies less than 12.4 miles (20 km) from mainland Papua New Guinea.

To the west, Papua New Guinea shares the island of New Guinea with the Indonesian province of Irian Jaya. The border separating the two was agreed upon by the Australian and Indonesian governments in 1968 without consultation with the local people. This border has been carefully mapped, but it crosses such rugged areas that little of its length of 482 miles (776 km) is patrolled effectively by either country.

Opposite: **Milne Bay harbor in the south, with the Owen Stanley Range in the background.**

Left: **Most of Papua New Guinea is forested and its villages have a remote character.**

7

The Papua New Guinea landscape ranges from rugged mountains, tropical jungles, and forested foothills to lowlands, savannah woodlands, mangrove swamps, and flat grasslands.

There is considerable evidence that people living in the center of New Guinea, including a group of anti-Indonesian guerrillas called the Free Papua Movement, can cross the political boundary at will, largely unhindered. To the east lie the Solomon Islands and to the north the Federated States of Micronesia.

The total area of Papua New Guinea is 178,656 square miles (462,840 square km), which is slightly larger than California. Of that land mass, about 85% is the mainland. The remaining 15% is made up of islands, the larger of which are New Britain and Bougainville. Some of these islands are the submerged eastern end of a curved mountain chain that begins in the Himalayas and continues through Malaysia and into the Pacific. Some of the islands are within the Pacific "ring of fire," an area of earthquakes and volcanic activity that forms a large circle in the Pacific Ocean. Others are coral atolls, islands formed by the accumulation of the exoskeletons of many generations of once-living coral. These atolls are usually ring- or horseshoe-shaped, and surround a shallow lagoon.

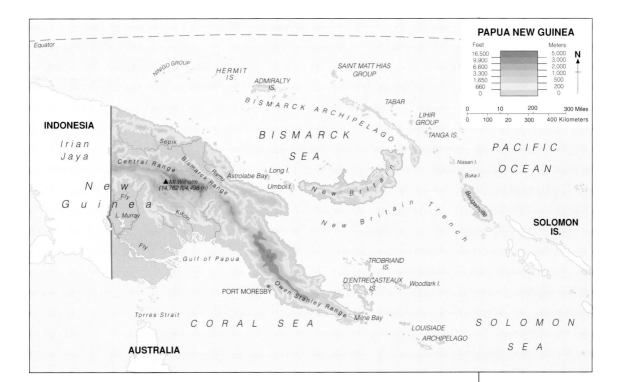

MOUNTAIN RANGES

The mainland is bisected from east to west by a spine of jagged and steep mountains reaching heights of over 13,000 feet (4,000 meters). Temporary paths were made over the mountains during World War II by factions involved in the fighting, but the range is not yet crossed by a permanent road. The only way to travel between north and south is by airplane, or on foot. Despite the isolation, the central highland valleys are among the most fertile and heavily populated areas of the country. The tribal people living there were not discovered by European explorers until as late as the 1930s, and they still maintain a largely traditional way of life. Many people have had little contact with the West, and European visitors are still a source of interest to the villagers.

In some areas the mountains graduate into rolling foothills extending to the sea, but elsewhere the coastline is largely fringed with mangroves. To the west are large, flat, and sparsely wooded grasslands with abundant rainfall and wildlife.

Despite the mountainous terrain, many towns are linked by roads. The building of such roads is a difficult and expensive operation. The longest road is the Highlands Highway, about 350 miles (563 km) long, running from Lae to Mt. Hagen in the central highlands.

FAST-FLOWING RIVERS

The mainland is laced with a network of rivers that flow from the central mountains toward the coast. The largest are the 700 mile (1,126 km) Sepik that runs toward the Bismarck Sea in the north, and the Fly that flows southward into the Gulf of Papua. These rivers are usually fastflowing and navigable and provide a useful alternative to the rough land routes.

The Sepik is bordered by large expanses of swamp for most of its length. There are few natural resources that can be exploited so there has been little development. The uppermost reaches of the Sepik, among the most isolated parts of the country, have seen little change and remain relatively untouched by Western influence. The Sepik region, which includes the river, its tributaries, and the surrounding villages, is well-populated and noted as a center for traditional art.

Houses and villages are found along the banks of the Sepik although huge expanses of swamp border parts of the river.

LIVING WITH VOLCANOES

Papua New Guinea lies within the volcanic and earthquake belt that circles the Pacific, running through Japan, Indonesia, New Zealand, and New Guinea. Volcanoes are an everpresent threat to the people who live near them, but fortunately they erupt infrequently, and well-planned emergency procedures can save entire populations.

Lava flows very slowly, but while people can outrun it, the lava can do much damage to forests, roads, and buildings. Falling ash can bury entire towns, but this normally happens over a period of time, and ashfall needs to be very thick before it becomes difficult for people to breathe.

On the morning of September 19, 1994, Tarvuvur and Vulcan, two volcanoes near Rabaul, erupted without warning. Violent explosions, poisonous gas, and a thick cloud of ash forced nearby residents to evacuate to safety. Vulcan ceased its activity in October that year, but explosions continued at Tarvuvur until March the following year. People were able to return to Rabaul in April 1995, and only one death—resulting from flooding brought about by the eruption—was recorded.

Despite the destruction they cause, volcanoes provide rich soils, and to farmers living in the area, this can be a benefit.

LEGACY OF GONDWANALAND

The island of New Guinea is thought to have once been a part of the super-continent of Gondwanaland which included Australia, Antarctica, Africa, and South America. The super-continent broke up about 65 million years ago and many of the plant and animal species found throughout Asia, Australia, the Pacific, and even Africa can be found in Papua New Guinea. There is much contrast between the mountains and low-lying areas because of the differences in temperature and rainfall, and different plant types have adapted to the conditions at each altitude.

The peaks of the highest mountains are occasionally white with snow, but this is the exception. Above 11,000 feet (3,350 meters), the mountains are covered with a type of alpine woodland that is very much like tundra in North America, with tussock grasses, low shrubs, tree ferns, southern pine, and native cedar. Many of the tiny flowers have close relatives as far away as the Himalayas and the European Alps. Lichens and mosses tint the landscape with spectacular hues of white, purple, gray, red, and pink. Some areas can be boggy, and rich organic soils like peat are widespread.

The landscape is similar to the highlands of New Zealand or Scotland, something unexpected on a tropical island. Farther down the slopes, at an altitude of between 11,000 and 6,600 feet (3,350 and 2,000 meters), are the montane forests where conifers and southern beech trees predominate, with an underlayer of large ferns and fungi. One tree can support up to 400 species of epiphytes (plants that live on the host plant but do not feed off them) such as orchids, mosses, and ferns.

Vegetation is thick throughout most of Papua New Guinea, but at the higher altitudes the trees grow stunted and twisted, matching the dark and gloomy atmosphere. Oak trees and pandanus (also called screw pines) are common, giving way to the lower montane forests at above 3,300 feet (1,000 meters) where hoop and klinkii pines, both valued for their timber, are dominant. Klinkii pines tower over the rest of the forest, reaching heights of over 280 feet (85 meters).

The valleys and lowlands that cover over 75% of Papua New Guinea are primarily tropical rainforest. Massive trees form a canopy and many

A group of people walking on a trail cut through a lowland forested area. Three-quarters of the country is covered with tropical rainforest.

"On the mainland alone, there may be as many as 20,000 species of flowering plant."

—Neil Nightingale, in his book New Guinea, an Island Apart

palm trees, bamboos, pandanus, and canes compete for sunlight. The plants grow rapidly with the high temperatures and ample water supply, and some trees reach 150 feet (45 meters) in height. Vines and climbers such as rattan and strangler figs add to the tangle of greenery. These are among the most fertile places in Papua New Guinea; in many valleys and on low slopes the villagers clear small patches of ground to grow sweet potatoes and bananas.

In the lowland regions, particularly around the rivers, are large areas of swampy woodlands. In some areas the grass floats on the constantly sodden earth. The residents harvest sago (a starchy palm used for food), wild sugarcane, and pit-pit (a sturdy cane used in the building of homes). At the western end of mainland Papua New Guinea and in the drier areas around Port Moresby the landscape becomes a savannah woodland similar to that in northern Australia. Dry grasses and thinly placed trees, mostly eucalypts, are found here.

New Guinea and Australia are thought to have been joined as recently as 6,000 years ago. It is not surprising then that they share many animal species, particularly marsupials (mammals whose young develop inside pouches found on their mothers' stomach). Wallabies, tree kangaroos, bandicoots, possums, and echidnas are found in both countries.

Pandanus nuts are highly valued and take some trouble to collect. People trudge for several days to lay claim to trees in the nutting season. The nuts are tough and heavy, and only a few clusters can be carried at a time. As a result the nuts are sparse in the markets and quite expensive.

COMMON BORDER

Neighboring Irian Jaya, with a population of nearly two million, is governed as part of Indonesia. Papua New Guinea, with its 4.4 million people, is an independent country. In 1968 the Australian and Indonesian governments drew a straight line down the New Guinea mainland to demarcate the national boundaries. Papua New Guinea was then under Australian administration. Today, many Papuan nationals living near the border still speak Bahasa Indonesia, the language of their neighbors.

Port Moresby is spread out around the coast and inland hills, and is the only major town in the southern part of the country. It is not connected by road to any other important town, and its geographical isolation is its main drawback.

COSMOPOLITAN CAPITAL

Port Moresby has a population of about 200,000, making it the country's largest town. Sited on a natural harbor, it was formerly the administrative headquarters of British New Guinea and remained so when the territory was amalgamated with Australian New Guinea after World War II. When the country gained its independence in 1975, Port Moresby's status as the capital became more meaningful. The central government offices, Parliament House, University of Papua New Guinea, National Museum and Art Gallery, and an international airport are located here.

The national buildings are mostly large, modern buildings on spacious grounds but Port Moresby has shantytowns too. Many people are lured into the city by the seemingly prosperous lifestyle, but many do not find it and end up living in squalid conditions among the squatters. Violence and crime are high and gangs of young male bandits called "rascals" operate all over the country; they are particularly active in impoverished areas with high unemployment.

REGIONAL CENTERS

LAE This city is located more centrally than Port Moresby and has a deeper natural harbor, making it a prosperous shipping center. It has road links with the fertile highlands (where cash crops like coffee and tea are grown), and has often been suggested as an alternative site for the nation's capital. However, it has a high proportion of unemployed people among its population of 90,000, and petty crime is prevalent.

Mt. Lunaman, a hill in the center of town, was the lookout point for the German and Japanese troops during World War II; it is riddled with tunnels and caves that are now occupied by the rascals. Formerly a supply center for goldmining, Lae was destroyed in the grim battles fought to expel the Japanese military during World War II but has been rebuilt farther inland.

In Lae, Papua New Guinea's second largest city, poverty exists alongside relative modernity.

MADANG With a population of about 30,000, it has often been called the prettiest town in the Pacific and is thus geared toward the tourist trade. It is a major northern coastal port that lost much of its business to Lae when the Highlands Highway, running from Lae to the central highlands, opened. However it has captured the area's logging trade to support its economy.

WEWAK AND GOROKA These two towns were formerly useful to the Europeans as trading points, pawns, and strategic locations during World War II. They have been able to thrive because of trade, attracting a large mix of cultural groups.

Pigs are an integral part of family life in Papua New Guinea.

ON THE LAND

Papua New Guinea has many varieties of snakes, including the poisonous death adder and taipan. Pigs were brought into Papua New Guinea about 6,000 years ago, most likely by immigrants or traders from various parts of Southeast Asia, and play an important part in the life of a village. They often live with the family, are spoken to, and given names. Women harvesting a new crop of sweet potatoes often lead them to the fields where they are let loose to root for remaining tubers. They are thus fed and help to till the soil, which must otherwise be done manually.

There is a New Guinea wild dog similar to the Australian dingo. It is seldom seen, but can be heard howling at night in the highest parts of Papua New Guinea. Domesticated dogs are kept as pets and to aid in hunting.

PROTECTED BY THE LAW

Early European traders were quick to exploit the unusual wildlife, paying local people to hunt for the spectacular and rare skins and feathers that were then exported and sold for a high price. This quickly decimated many species on islands where no large carnivorous predators exist.

Much of Papua New Guinea's wildlife has now been recognized as a valuable asset, and many have been declared "national animals" since the 1920s and protected by legislation. This means they can only be hunted by traditional methods for tribal use. Animals are considered to belong to the people on whose land they are found. Tribal landowners whose existence is inextricably tied to their surroundings usually have traditions and laws that conserve the natural resources on which they depend for their livelihood. Commercial and sport hunting of these animals is illegal and the penalties for transgressors are stiff.

IN THE AIR

Papua New Guinea is recognized as having one of the richest and most diverse bird populations in the world, and many of the birds have been declared national animals. There are more species of kingfishers, pigeons, and parrots here than anywhere else. Other birds include hornbills, big palm cockatoos, and cassowaries. The birds feast on the fruits, nuts, nectar, and pollen that in other countries are eaten by monkeys and other primates or squirrels. The most famous bird, appearing on the country's flag and coat of arms, is the beautifully plumed bird of paradise. Of the 43 species of this bird, 38 are found in Papua New Guinea. Its feathers can be seen in the elaborate headdresses of the indigenous people.

Perhaps most spectacular of all of Papua New Guinea's fauna are the insects. The largest of all moths, with a wing span of over 38 square inches (250 square cm), is the Hercules moth. There are also giant millipedes, a stick insect that reaches over 12 inches (30 cm) in length, and the breathtaking birdwing butterflies. Of the 11 birdwing species documented, eight are found in Papua New Guinea. The female Queen Alexandra's Birdwing has a wing span of up to 12 inches (30 cm). A curious insect found only in northern Australia and Papua New Guinea is the antlered fly. In males of this fiercely territorial species a large antler-like structure protruding from their heads is used as a defensive display. Some insects, such as green scarab beetles, are used by the natives as body ornaments. Many of the unusual insects are now being collected and bred to ensure their conservation.

The bird of paradise is found mainly in the New Guinea highlands and on nearby islands. It is the adult male of the species that boasts beautiful plumage.

The waters surrounding Papua New Guinea nurture beautiful marine life and coral reefs.

IN THE WATER

The coastal areas are lined with swampy marshes teeming with plants that have adapted to living in the salty tidal conditions. They act as a haven for fish and prawns to breed, and in some areas the trees can grow up to 100 feet (30 meters) high. The sea water is often heavily silted because of the steep slopes and high rainfall that flow into the rivers and sea. Although the low visibility annoys divers, many of whom consider Papua New Guinea one of the best dive sites in the world, it provides the ideal habitat for sea grass, a land plant that has adapted to living in the sea. It grows where the water is too deep for mangroves but too murky for coral, and supports a huge number of sea creatures, including the dugong, or sea cow.

Several varieties of marine turtle are caught by the coastal people: the green turtle for its meat and the hawksbill for its shell. Fly River has its own tube-nosed turtle, which can be seen on the country's five-toea coin. Whales, dolphins, corals, venomous sea snakes, and an abundance of yet unclassified marine creatures fascinate divers and marine biologists alike.

ENDANGERED SEA COWS

Dugongs are thought to be one of the creatures that early European sailors mistook for mermaids. These sea cows, as they are commonly called, are large marine mammals that can grow to nine feet (2.7 meters) in length, and a male can weigh up to a ton (0.9 tonnes). They inhabit shallow coastal waters and are herbivorous, docile in nature, and slow-moving. Sea grass is the dugong's primary food. An adult dugong may need to eat up to 88 pounds (40 kg) of sea grass to meet its daily food requirement.

The animals live in pairs or in small groups. They can stay underwater for only two or three minutes before surfacing for air, when they become relatively easy targets for hunters. Dugongs are prized in Papua New Guinea and elsewhere for their meat, blubber, skin, tusk-like incisors, and oil. They can no longer be found in many of their former haunts and are now considered endangered, with less than 40,000 of them left in the world.

WET, HOT, AND HUMID

Temperatures are high in most of Papua New Guinea's lowland areas and along the coast, averaging 81°F (27°C). The highland areas are much cooler at about 68°F (20°C).

For the most part, the country experiences two main seasons, the wet and the dry. However, there is so much rain in some areas that the land is not dry at all, but merely less rain-sodden. The northwest monsoon brings rain from December to March, and southeasterly trade winds blow from May to October, bringing drier and cooler weather. The in-between months of April and November are the most uncomfortable, being hot and humid without the cooling relief of rain.

The rainy period varies greatly from one region to another, as the mountains tend to capture much of the precipitation, sheltering some areas from the monsoonal rain. The Port Moresby area has a definite dry season, with an annual average rainfall of 39 inches (1,000 mm) that falls in short bursts during the wet season. In Lae, the average rainfall is 177 inches (4,500 mm), falling mostly between May and October, with the wettest months being June, July, and August. In some areas (the western part of New Britain, parts of the Gulf of Papua, and some of the western provinces) the rain falls all year round, and rainfall can average over 236 inches (6000 mm) per year.

Despite heavy rainfall in the rest of the country, the capital city of Port Moresby is much drier. The effect is particularly evident during the dry season from May to October, when the city suffers extended droughts and has to impose strict water rationing.

HISTORY

THERE ARE NO WRITTEN RECORDS of Papua New Guinea's history before the arrival of European explorers several hundred years ago. The country is a collection of vastly different cultural groups; until as recently as the 1930s some still had a Stone Age-like existence, using only tools made of stone and wood. Nevertheless, a complex social structure exists within each group. The prehistory of Papua New Guinea has been pieced together largely by archeologists and anthropologists.

It is widely thought that the first people on the New Guinea mainland arrived as immigrants from the eastern Indonesian islands as early as 50,000 years ago, in the glacial period. Later arrivals came from other areas in Indonesia, Asia, and the South Pacific. These people were hunters and gatherers and were most likely nomadic. Although New Guinea probably was once connected to Australia, part of the immigrants' journey involved crossing deep sea waters in canoes.

It is highly probable that new agricultural methods were introduced by farmers arriving from Southeast Asia. As tools were developed and new crops introduced, bigger groups of people settled in fixed locations. Archeological discoveries include drainage channels that indicate the existence of agriculture around 9,000 years ago. Trenched roads, defensive gates, and ditches used for fighting have also been found in the southern highlands, indicating that these ancient tribes were often at war with each other. Between 17,000 and 10,000 years ago, climatic warming led to a worldwide melting of ice sheets, leading to a gradual rise in sea levels which covered the original land links with Australia. The grasslands decreased in size and the forested areas increased.

Above and opposite: **From ancient to modern times, dugout canoes have been used for transporting people and cargo. They are made by hollowing out a tree trunk by burning, chipping, and scraping. They still provide a useful means of travel for tribal people living along the coast.**

FARMERS AND TRADERS 10,000 YEARS AGO

About 9,000 years ago, large parts of the Wahgi swamp areas in the Western Highlands were drained to create productive farming land, an achievement remarkable for its time.

Evidence suggests that New Guinea highlanders may have been among the world's first agriculturalists, growing crops of yams, bananas, and coconuts. The early farmers developed sophisticated techniques to obtain maximum yields without the use of metal tools, including composting dead vegetation to add nutrients to the soil, and a system of crop rotation.

Despite fighting between clans and villages, trade was carried out on a small scale. Long before Europeans arrived, overland and inter-island trade routes existed for sago, pottery, shells, salt, and stone axes. Large seagoing trade expeditions called *hiri* ("hih-REE") were launched by the Motu in the Port Moresby area, who traded pots for sago and canoe logs in the Gulf of Papua. More recently, in the past 1,000 years, trade with Asia has increased. Chinese merchants and sea captains were the middlemen in trade that exchanged Asian glass beads, metal goods, cloth, and porcelain for the New Guinea tree bark, spices, and exotic bird feathers.

Steel axes, which preceded the arrival of European settlers, were traded inland. They were more efficient than stone axes in clearing gardens and making canoes. This increased leisure time for the men, leading to more frequent tribal wars.

TRIBE OR CLAN AS BASIC SOCIAL UNIT

Unlike other parts of the world, the development of agriculture in what is now Papua New Guinea did not result in the growth of larger political and social units such as cities and states; instead the tribe or clan remained the basic social unit. This was because the basic food crops could not be stored for long periods of time due to climatic conditions, so farming was a fulltime activity. It was not possible to stockpile food to create wealth, or fight protracted wars to conquer neighboring territories. Short and ferocious battles were fought over territory and property, but these were conducted mainly in the valleys, with villages built defensively on the hillsides.

EUROPEAN ARRIVAL

Written history in Papua New Guinea began in 1526, when the Portuguese sea captain Jorge de Meneses sighted the coast and named it *Illpas dos Papuas* (Land of the Frizzy-haired People). He was unimpressed with what he found—a difficult terrain with no apparent spices or natural wealth to encourage exploration. The Spaniard Inigo Ortiz de Retes landed on the northeastern parts of the mainland in 1545, and named the land Nueva Guinea (New Guinea), because it reminded him of the Guinea Coast in Africa. Despite a superficial interest in the island, it was largely ignored by explorers as it lay away from the direct sea routes used at the time.

Fierce battles sometimes broke out between the villagers and the Europeans over traditional land areas that were taken by force.

The first European attempt at settlement, made in 1793, was led by Captain John Hayes, who claimed the entire island of New Guinea for Britain. He built a fortified settlement that he called Fort Coronation at the western end of New Guinea. It was used for trading in nutmeg trees, dyewood roots, and teak. The settlement was abandoned the following year after it was flooded by monsoonal rains, attacked by hostile locals, and plagued by tropical mosquito-borne diseases. The Dutch disputed the British claim, and in 1828 laid claim to the western half of New Guinea. As before, the settlers were plagued with mosquitoes and the threat of malaria, and Fort du Bus was deserted in 1835. The Dutch continued to claim sovereignty over the western half of New Guinea, but were in reality too distant to monitor the territory.

Traders based in Australia were the next to show interest in New Guinea. Whalers and sealers traded small axes, rum, beads, mirrors, and firearms in exchange for pearls, tortoiseshell, coconuts, hardwood, rubber, feathers, and copra. In some areas used regularly by trading vessels, the local population became accustomed to the traders and learned to barter. Other areas were taken by force. By the second quarter of the 19th century, most of New Guinea's coastline had been charted.

From the 1840s, parts of New Guinea, Milne Bay, and the Bismarck Archipelago became recruiting points for people supplying cheap labor to sugar plantations in Fiji, Samoa, and Australia. Most of the plantations had slave-like conditions and the workers, called "blackbirds," were exploited. Around this time Christian missionaries began to visit New Guinea and the surrounding islands; their influence is reflected in the high percentage of Christians in Papua New Guinea today.

In 1884 Germany claimed the northeastern area of New Guinea and the Bismarck Archipelago, setting up a trading post about 300 miles (480 km) up the Sepik River. Fearing a German move south toward their own coastline, the Australian colonies, then independent of each other, collectively pressured the British government to make its presence felt more strongly. That same year the southeastern portion of New Guinea was annexed by Britain. Many villagers were unhappy with foreign rule; fierce battles ensued, and the villagers were ultimately defeated.

THE DIFFICULTIES OF EXPLORATION

Very little of the Papuan mainland was explored by Europeans before World War I because of a logistics problem. A porter could only carry up to 40 pounds (18 kilograms) of food, enough for one person to live on for 14 days, but this would not have been able to sustain prolonged European exploration of the area. A relay network was soon set up in which teams of porters ferried food and supplies to inland stores, venturing as far into the mainland as was logistically possible; such a system had its limitations. The use of planes to airdrop food ended this restriction, and there was a boom in successful exploration from the 1920s.

LIFE IN THE COLONIES

The German colony was initially administered by the New Guinea Kompagnie, a trading company accorded the task of developing whatever land it could acquire on behalf of the German government. Germany still passed the laws for the new territory, but its administration, development, and local matters were entrusted to the Kompagnie. The company's main concern was profit; it established tobacco plantations in Astrolabe Bay and coconut plantations elsewhere.

The German government took over the Kompagnie's rule in 1899 and for the most part the colony continued to be run for its plantations and trade value. The focus was on building roads and setting up administrative controls, but little was done for the local people who provided cheap labor for the German operations. Each village was required to nominate a *luluai* ("loo-loo-AY," or headman) authorized to collect taxes, settle minor disputes, report major disputes, and ensure that the villagers obeyed government orders. *Luluais* were assisted by *tultuls* ("TUHL-tuhls") who

Village chiefs; under German rule they helped maintain order among the villagers.

25

New Guineans under German colonial control were treated with disdain. They were expected to call all white people Masta *("MAS-tah") or* Misis *("MISS-sis"), while a New Guinean male was addressed as* boi *("BOY"). They had to stand up when spoken to by a European and step aside when meeting a white person in the street.*

acted as interpreters and go-betweens. By 1908 the coconut plantations were maturing, copra exports boomed, and scientific expeditions were starting to penetrate the inhospitable interior. By that time most of the territory was under the control of government stations and district officers. Germany lost the colony in 1914 when it was occupied by Australian forces. It was renamed the Territory of New Guinea when Australia was given mandate over it by the League of Nations in 1921.

The southeastern area of New Guinea, including Port Moresby, was annexed by the British in 1884. Like the Germans, the immediate British concern was to set up a governmental infrastructure within the new colony. Its administrative structure was similar to that of the Germans, only instead of having *luluais*, the British installed "constables." The area was divided into three divisions, each governed by a regional magistrate. The British protectorate was handed over to Australia in 1906, when it was renamed Papua. After World War I, Australia continued to govern both Papua and the Territory of New Guinea. Administrative control was based in Australia, where all the major decisions were made; these were then implemented by a mostly expatriate Australian staff located in Port Moresby and Rabaul.

GOLD RUSH

In the 1920s gold was found at Wau and Bulolo, and the exploration of the highlands began in earnest. The fledgling use of airplanes in the supply network meant that expeditions could venture into more rugged territory than previously possible. Around this time, the New Guinea highland peoples were discovered when a couple of Australian gold prospectors stumbled into a valley. They were astonished to find a civilization untouched by the outside world, and numbering close to one million people. Despite the flurry of activity caused by gold mining, little infrastructural development took place during the three decades preceding World War II.

CAUGHT UP IN A FOREIGNERS' WAR

World War II arrived in the Papua and New Guinea territories in 1942. The invading Japanese planned to take Port Moresby and set it up as their southern outpost in Southeast Asia and the Pacific, to supply raw materials such as tin, rubber, and oil. The Japanese invasion was swift; the army quickly captured much of New Guinea's north coast and most of the surrounding islands. The Australian and American forces held on to Milne Bay and a few offshore islands, such as the Trobriands. However, the Japanese victory was shortlived. They came close to their original goal of Port Moresby, but were driven back by Australian forces at Kokoda. By September 1942 the Japanese had started their long, slow retreat. It took the Allied forces until 1945 to recover all of the mainland, and some islands were not reclaimed by Australian forces until after the atomic bombings of Hiroshima and Nagasaki.

The war fought in Papua New Guinea was a particularly grim one. The soldiers traveled through the rugged and seemingly impassable terrain largely on foot and with minimal supplies. By 1942 the warring countries took to the air in an attempt to hasten their victories, starting a series of bombing raids that continued for three years. The devastating effects of war were widely felt by the local people—the bombardment of their towns and villages resulted in the destruction of canoes, trees, plants, and animals that they depended on for their livelihood. The danger of aerial attack and military restrictions on sea travel limited coastal fishing. The scarcity of food and other raw materials added to the hardship of living in a country at war.

Soldiers evacuating an injured member during World War II. The Australians fought the advancing Japanese troops in Papua New Guinea.

An estimated 55,000 indigenous Papuans and New Guineans were involved in World War II as carriers, stretcher bearers, laborers, and guides.

27

The Australian administration of the territory of Papua and New Guinea faced the challenge of honoring promises it had made to respect local customs and safeguard traditionally owned land while providing profit incentives to attract Europeans with expertise and capital.

TOWARD INDEPENDENCE

In 1945 Australian Colonel Jack Keith Murray was named the chief administrator of both territories, now called the Territory of Papua and New Guinea. His task was to establish health and education services, control local disputes, and liaise with plantation owners.

From 1946 Australia administered the territories as a United Nations mandate. Soon after, the push toward independence was set in motion. The First House of Assembly was formed with 64 members in 1964. This was replaced in 1968 with the Second House of Assembly with 94 members. The Second House decided that the independent country would be known as Papua New Guinea. It set up a committee in 1972 to draft a constitution, and the Third House of Assembly was formed. On October 1, 1973 the territory obtained full self-government and on September 16, 1975 the new constitution took effect. Australia's Prime Minister Gough Whitlam and Britain's Prince Charles attended the official change of flags, along with a crowd of 10,000 people in a stadium in Port Moresby.

POST INDEPENDENCE

Not everyone in Papua New Guinea agreed that independence was a good thing. There was the problem of creating a sense of loyalty to the central government, located far away in Port Moresby. To the people, the highlanders in particular, the government seemed removed from the day-to-day issues affecting them. In a sense, people in the remote villages were fearful of being dominated by others with a lifestyle that was more advanced. There was still some resentment regarding earlier governments' attempts to outlaw traditional practices such as cannibalism, and some areas of the country were officially barred to travelers because of possible hostility by the tribespeople. Since independence, the establishment of local governments and village courts has done much to ease the tension.

However, the failure to create a sense of national identity has resulted in numerous separatist movements that flare up periodically. Josephine Abijah, the only woman in the 109-member parliament, pushed for the southern region of Papua to break away from the rest of the country and declare its independence. She was supported by wealthy business people who did not want to share their region's affluence with the rest of the country.

District or provincial officers go deep into the mountainous areas to educate villagers on modern ways. They explain about the government and how it wants to keep diseases in check and help the people grow better crops. The officers face the possibility of attack from tribal warriors and have to work hard to win their trust.

NATIONAL FLAG

The flag of Papua New Guinea was formally adopted in 1971. It is based on a design by a 15-year-old student, Susan Karike, winner of a national flag-design competition. Black, red, and yellow are traditional colors. The yellow bird of paradise, which features widely in tribal activities, soars above the Southern Cross, symbolizing the country's evolution into nationhood. The Southern Cross, a constellation found in the southern hemisphere, signifies Papua New Guinea's historical links with Australia and its goodwill toward its South Pacific neighbors.

A Bougainville rebel prepares for a fight against government forces.

TROUBLE ON BOUGAINVILLE

The secessionist movement on Bougainville island continues to be a political issue. Its proponents argue that the island holds stronger cultural and geographic ties with the Solomon Islands than with New Guinea. Of considerable significance is the fact that in 1964 Panguna, on Bougainville island, was the site of a major copper discovery and over K400 million (US$288 million) was invested in the development of the mine and the surrounding infrastructure including roads, a new town, a power station, and a seaport. By the time Papua New Guinea gained its independence, the mine was earning half of the country's internal revenue.

When the secessionist movement headed by Father John Momis escalated, negotiations were held. The secessionists were assured they would exert a strong influence on the rest of the country and were allowed to set up the first provincial government. Thus persuaded, they reluctantly chose to remain within the jurisdiction of the National Parliament and things appeared well for a short time.

In the 14 years from Papua New Guinea's independence in 1975 to Bougainville Copper's closure in 1989, Bougainville Copper provided a massive 20% of the government's total revenue.

A small group of traditional landowners were enjoying huge royalties from mining, but little community development resulted. There was growing suspicion among the people that they had been shortchanged in their earliest negotiations with Bougainville Copper Limited's parent company, CRA. In 1987 the Panguna Landowners Association was formed, led by Perpetua Sereo and Francis Ona. It demanded stricter environmental measures, backpayments in profits, and US$10 billion in compensation. When the CRA failed to meet these demands, the Bougainville Revolutionary Army began to sabotage the mine, which was closed in May 1989. This was a blow to Papua New Guinea's economy, partially offset by Ok Tedi and other highland gold mines. A state of emergency was declared and the situation deteriorated into civil war.

Early in 1997 the prime minister, Sir Julius Chan, and a few cabinet ministers hired a London-based mercenary group, Sandline Limited, at a cost of about K51 million (US$37 million), to fight the Bougainville insurgents. Neither parliament nor the people were consulted. In March Brigadier-General Jerry Singirok, who spoke against the move, was sacked for insubordination. The issue aroused national outrage marked by violence in the capital. Riot police were sent in, the Sandline contract was suspended, and the prime minister and his deputy resigned.

Sir Julius Chan was pressured into stepping down from office when his contract with foreign mercenaries, paid to fight the Bougainville insurgents, turned popular opinion against him.

MOVE TOWARD PEACE

Meetings between Bougainville factions to address the crisis have since been held on neutral territory in New Zealand. A document called the Burnham Declaration is being formulated; it recommends a ceasefire, total demilitarization of the area, and the establishment of a United Nations peacekeeping force. Both the newly elected government of Bill Skate, the country's current prime minister, and the Bougainville Revolutionary Army have publicly endorsed the recommendations and further peace talks are being planned.

GOVERNMENT

PAPUA NEW GUINEA IS AN INDEPENDENT STATE and a constitutional monarchy at the same time. The situation is the same as in countries such as Canada, New Zealand, and Australia. Independence means that Papua New Guinea is self-governing, makes its own laws, and has its own government. Yet it is a member of the British Commonwealth, with the British monarch as its head of state. The monarch, currently Queen Elizabeth II, is represented within the country by a governor-general, whose role is primarily ceremonial. The governor-general must be a citizen of Papua New Guinea.

The nation's democratic structure rests on a popular vote and the right of parliament to lodge a motion of no confidence in the ruling government, resulting in a new election. The 1975 constitution vests executive power in the National Executive Council headed by the prime minister, who is the leader of the majority party in the single-chamber National Parliament. The prime minister subsequently chooses ministers from within his or her political party or coalition of parties.

Opposite: **Parliament House in Port Moresby is built in the style of a traditional spirit house.**

POWER OF VETO

The National Parliament is the top rung of a three-tiered government system similar to that of Australia: national, provincial, and local. Elections are held not more than five years apart. Citizens over the age of 18 are eligible to vote and stand for office in the 109-member parliament, and in the provincial and local assemblies.

The National Parliament holds ultimate authority over the provincial and local governments and can vote to veto laws made by those bodies that it decides are not in the best interests of the country. It can also suspend those governments in cases of gross mismanagement. The constitution can only be altered by the National Parliament in two votes of 72 or more members, in two sessions held no less than six weeks apart. The National Parliament is housed in Port Moresby, the National Capital District.

POWER TO THE PEOPLE: DECENTRALIZATION

The system of decentralized provincial government was introduced in 1976 to quell secessionist uprisings on some of the islands.

Papua New Guinea's constitution recognizes the importance of involving people at all levels of society in decision-making to provide a sense of cohesion. Hence the adoption of provincial and local governments.

Apart from the National Capital District, which is Port Moresby, there are 19 provinces throughout the country, each with a provincial assembly, executive council, and centrally appointed governor who represents the provincial government in the same way that the prime minister heads the national government. The provinces are Central, Oro, Milne Bay, Morobe, Madang, Manus, North Solomons, East Sepik, Western, Sandaun, Gulf, Eastern Highlands, Western Highlands, Southern Highlands, Simbu, Enga, East New Britain, West New Britain, and New Ireland.

The provincial governments deal with social, health, and educational matters, and the establishment of village courts in their own regions. They also provide input to the National Parliament on issues relating to community development, mass communications, and the establishment of provincial courts. The provincial governments are funded by a variety of grants from the national government, as well as taxes from retail sales and the issue of gambling and liquor licenses.

LOCAL COUNCILS

The local councils represent the most fundamental level of government. Over 160 councils preside over issues of regional concern. In isolated areas the councils are more relevant to the populace than a faraway political body. The councils are responsible for the maintenance of roads, bridges, and markets, the provision of fresh water, sanitation, and public transportation services, and the smooth operation of airfields, and postal and other communications in isolated areas. To fund their activities, registration fees are charged on items such as bicycles and dogs, and taxes are levied on land ownership and cash wages.

COURT SYSTEM

The judicial system of Papua New Guinea is similar to the U.S. and Australian models. A judge decides the outcome of a case after hearing legal representation from both sides, while more serious crimes are brought before a jury. There are several levels in the court system. The Supreme Court is the country's highest court and the final court of appeal, having the authority to interpret and enforce the constitution. Usually three judges sit together during a hearing in this court. The National Court has unlimited jurisdiction, involving a single judge sitting for each hearing. District courts and local courts have more limited powers and are presided over by fulltime magistrates. Finally, the village courts hear cases such as robbery or assault within the village. The magistrates are chosen by the village people and no legal qualifications are required.

Other sections of the judicial system include land courts which settle disputes over traditional land ownership, and administrative bodies that control the appointment of judges and magistrates. The discretionary use

The village court magistrate is elected from within the village and need not have legal qualifications. As a result, the rulings of the village court sometimes reflect the local standards of what is considered proper behavior, even if these are different from national law.

of the death penalty was introduced in 1991 for crimes of rape or murder. The courts are kept busy, particularly with the problem of petty crimes committed by the rascals. Records show that in 1990, the National Court heard more than 1,500 cases and an estimated 120,000 cases were heard in the district and local courts.

Corruption within the government is another issue that has plagued the country since independence. There is a courtlike organization called the Leadership Tribunal to examine charges of corruption against elected officials. In 1991 Deputy Prime Minister Ted Diro and Governor-General Sir Vincent Serei Eri were compelled by the tribunal to resign when Diro was found guilty of corruption and Eri refused to remove him from office.

The assemblies and courts of law in Papua New Guinea are uniquely placed as a significant portion of their participants cannot read or write and speak mutually incomprehensible languages. The provision of interpreters and audio recordings of procedures means that more people can be engaged in the legal and political operation of their community.

Chieftains such as this one from the Trobriand Islands have a responsibility to ensure that their tribal members conform to government laws.

LAW AND ORDER

The age-old custom of intertribal fighting and the seeking of vengeance have not been wiped out entirely, especially among tribes in the more remote areas that have had little contact with outsiders. Although warriors who kill in tribal warfare can be tried in a court of law, a village will not necessarily cooperate in the arrest of one of its members. Tribal custom does not regard this as a breakdown of order, but the process by which the ancient rules of law and order are being implemented. As long as a man's action does not affect his own village negatively, his tribe usually does not regard his action as being wrong or deserving of punishment. A man who will never cheat someone in his village, for example, may be proud of robbing someone from a rival tribe. So rules of behavior that are upheld within a community will not necessarily be upheld outside it.

HIGH TURNOVER OF POLITICIANS

To win a seat at any level of government a candidate must win a majority of votes, even if only 10% of the voters vote. This has on occasion led to disenchantment and claims of corruption and bias, with dissatisfaction spilling over into post-election violence. Few members have the ongoing popular support to last more than one term in parliament, and the high turnover of politicians leads to a dearth of experience and continuity within parliament.

Unlike the U.S. or Australian systems, the candidates do not stand for election on an ideological platform, but rely on their personality and regional ties to secure votes. Once in parliament they decide which alliance or party they want to support. The politicians are free to change their party allegiance at any time, depending on the issue being debated and the charisma of the main proponents. In trying to achieve a majority vote on any issue each party attempts to lure members into its camp, and much of a politician's time is spent in political maneuvering, forming and breaking alliances. The drawback is that the shifting alliances of party members causes much instability.

The country's first prime minister, Michael Somare, was faced with the task of building a nation from a great diversity of cultures and languages.

PRIME MINISTERS SINCE INDEPENDENCE

1975	Michael T. Somare (Pangu Pati)
1980	Sir Julius Chan (People's Progress Party)
1982	Michael T. Somare (Pangu Pati)
1985	Paias Wingti (People's Democratic Movement)
1988	Rabbie Namaliu (Pangu Pati)
1992	Paias Wingti (People's Democratic Movement)
1994	Sir Julius Chan (People's Progress Party)
1997	Bill Skate (People's National Congress)

The prime minister is elected by majority vote in parliament, and is usually the chosen leader of the majority party, or of the coalition, an alliance formed by mutual agreement between two or more groups with different interests. There is remarkable ideological consensus between the political parties, with only the best means to the end being debated. However, the continually shifting web of alliances means that any prime minister committed to reform is unable to take tough measures if he or she wishes to remain in power.

Changes in legislation do not necessarily affect the ruling government's policies and the National Parliament can challenge the government with a vote of no confidence. Fortunately, the government is protected from such a motion for the first 18 months. This time frame was formerly six months, but the rapid changing of governments meant that very little could be achieved by any leader. While this shows up the inefficiency of the system, it also means that no political group in the country is powerful enough to stage a military coup.

Rabbie Namaliu, prime minister from 1988 to 1992, was one of the figures in Papua New Guinea's volatile political scene.

It is perhaps surprising that a nation made up of people and leaders with such great differences in culture and language, and with an entrenched system of intertribal hostilities, can function smoothly. In a debate in the House of Assembly, for example, there is no common language and interpreters have to be relied on. Yet, in spite of the difficulties, the country operates under a single united and democratic government. In this respect Papua New Guinea has succeeded where some developing nations have failed.

NATIONAL DEFENSE

The Papua New Guinea defense force was created in 1973 while operating under the auspices of the Australian defense force. When its command was internalized in Papua New Guinea in 1975 it was merged into a single unified force. It does not have separate army, navy, and air forces but consists of three distinct operational elements: land, maritime, and air; these are supported by training, maintenance, transport, and supply units within the force.

The Papua New Guinea defense force has been employed both internally and externally. Within the country it patrols the border with Irian Jaya to prevent border crossings by rebels. Its external involvement arose in 1980 when it was deployed to put down a secessionist movement on Espiritu Santo, an island in the southwest Pacific. On more than one occasion, it has been used alongside the Papua New Guinea police force to maintain control during local uprisings, such as the insurrection movement on Bougainville and when civil unrest arose in Port Moresby in 1985 because of political tensions.

HELP FOR CIVILIANS

It is estimated that males fit for military service number nearly 636,000. In peacetime the Papua New Guinea defense force contributes its services to the civilian populace. The land element collects topographical information to compile more accurate maps; it also carries out small-scale building and repairs to village facilities such as water tanks and school buildings. The engineering battalion designs and constructs airfields, bridges, and roads in remote areas. Mass immunization and hygiene education programs are carried out throughout the country by the preventative medicine platoon, which occasionally provides other medical support in remote areas. The maritime and air elements assist with civilian search and rescue operations, medical evacuations, and the coastal surveillance of illegal fishing.

ECONOMY

A LARGE PART OF PAPUA NEW GUINEA'S POPULATION still lives in a largely non-wage system. Up to 72% of the people make their living through subsistence farming, obtaining other goods through barter. However, the need for cash is slowly catching on as there are taxes to be paid and purchases for clothes, beer, tobacco, rice, and canned fish to be made. Money is also required to send children to school.

There is a growing need for wage-earning jobs as the population grows and more people are educated and become potentially employable, but the number of job opportunities remains low. About a fifth of those who work for wages are employed in government service (based largely on the Australian model), and the remainder in mining for multinational companies, plantations, service industries, and limited manufacturing. This sector is supported mainly by export earnings, with the principal exports being gold, copper, coffee, cocoa, palm oil, silver, and forestry products.

The minimum wage set for urban workers is nearly three times that of their rural counterparts.

Left and opposite: **Those who once worked only at home now welcome employment as a means to earn much-needed cash.**

Ok Tedi, located high in the central mountains near the border with Irian Jaya, has rich gold and copper deposits. The mining project bears the name of the local river, Ok Tedi, and the Ok Tedi Mining Company is a consortium formed by the government of Papua New Guinea with Australian, American, and German multinational companies.

PLENTIFUL NATURAL RESOURCES

Papua New Guinea's hopes of economic development rest on its vast resources of minerals, oils, and natural gas. Mining contributes about 60% of the country's export income and also provides about 40% of the country's internal revenue through a system of taxes and government-owned shares. Gold and copper compete as the country's biggest earners, depending on fluctuations in world commodity markets. Oil, gas, nickel, silver, and other minerals are the targets for extensive exploration and mining. The government has bargained shrewdly with the multinationals that invest in the various mining projects, winning government and local shareholdings and significant compensation for traditional landowners.

MINING REGULATIONS

Papua New Guinea law provides for 1.25% of a mine's gross export sales to be paid in royalties, 20% of which goes to the traditional landowners and the remainder to the government (which, in turn, gives the provincial government a grant from national revenue). The landowners are provided with equity in the mining company, and compensation is paid to them according to a set schedule. This is based on the area of land affected, the number of trees cut, the gardens destroyed, and fish and other wildlife driven away as a result of mining activities. In addition, the mine is usually required to offer contracts for spin-off businesses to the local people.

Each mine must negotiate other agreements in a forum, and proposals concerning the relocation of housing or education near a mine must be agreed upon before mining can proceed. Despite this often laborious process, ongoing mining operations can cause much dissatisfaction, spilling over into civil unrest. Ok Tedi's continued dumping of toxic waste into the Fly River, leading to environmental degradation, is an example.

An employee of the Ok Tedi project relaxes outside his home with his family. The Ok Tedi mining community has found itself transported from a Stone Age village lifestyle into the modern era with its television sets, computers, helicopters, and bulldozers.

Commercial logging of klinkii pines is carried out by foreign companies. Once the valuable timber has been removed, the remainder is often burned to free the land for farming.

UNTAPPED FISHERIES AND EXPLOITED FORESTS

Fishing has always been a significant activity in this country with about 8,300 km (5,154 miles) of coastline, large rivers, and over 600 islands. It is practiced mainly by coastal villagers using traditional methods, a few foreign trawlers licensed to fish in the waters, and a fleet of tuna boats. The tropical waters support a variety of fish including tuna, spanish mackerel, and barramunda. The lack of processing and canning facilities, however, means that this resource is not fully exploited to feed the population.

Forestry has been carried out since before independence. Inadequate laws and lack of monitoring by the authorities have resulted in virgin forests being torn apart with little regard for the environment. Such destruction has resulted in land erosion, rivers choked with silt, and a loss of wildlife. It has also affected the rural people who use forest resources for building, food, and medicine. Nonetheless, forestry has long been an export earner with a large variety of high quality hardwoods being harvested. These are sold as logs, lumber, and woodchips.

MANUFACTURING

Manufacturing remains a weak area of the economy despite the government's attempts to promote expansion. The problems include a largely unskilled labor force, low productivity, relatively high minimum wages in the urban areas (compared with those in some Asian countries), limited cash resources in the economy, a limited local market to sell to, and competition against cheap imports (because of the strength of the kina against external markets).

Papua New Guinea produces beverages and processed foods on a small scale for domestic consumption, but still imports most of its food items.

The isolation of many communities means that the high cost of transporting goods in or out outweighs the local desire to have them. One area of concern is the country's dependence on imported food. Around 50% of Papua New Guinea's total imports is made up of food items, some of which the nation could reasonably be producing itself; canned fish is an example. The difficulty seems to be the lack of local capital to establish industrial facilities, along with a deep-seated reluctance to accept an industry largely funded by overseas investors.

Some processing of export agricultural items such as coffee, palm oil, and timber takes place, and there are a few clothing and metal fabrication factories. Beer, cigarettes, and soft drinks have been produced in the country since before independence, and a sugar industry was developed in the early 1980s. To protect the local sugar industry, sugar imports are now banned. Papua New Guinea is self-sufficient in chicken and chicken-based products, and meat canneries have been established in Madang and Port Moresby, but these are not enough to sustain a whole country that is chronically deficient in sources of protein.

FARMING

It is estimated that over 1.5 million Papuans, or over a third of the population, are farmers. There are distinct areas of work: subsistence farming, the small-scale cultivation of food for sale in the markets, and cash cropping. Subsistence farming means that a family grows only enough food to feed themselves. Cash cropping is the cultivation of crops like coffee and palm oil for sale. Unlike other developing nations that rely heavily on single cash crops and suffer repercussions when the crop fails or when the world market crashes, Papuan farmers have a strong subsistence base to fall back on. Many villagers are flexible and discerning enough to move into cash cropping when the need arises (for example to pay a child's school fees). Once the need for cash is met, they devote their energies to something else. Village root crops (sweet potatoes, yams, and taro) grow efficiently, producing a high yield of food energy per unit of work put into their cultivation (up to four times as much as that of rice) so that time and energy can be devoted to other crops or projects at the same time.

An agricultural worker tends to vegetables at a commercial farm.

While much of the country's agriculture is carried out successfully by individuals on small plots of land, there are about 650 estates or plantations of over 125 acres (50 hectares) each. While some are owned by local capitalists, many church missions derive a significant portion of their operating revenues from such plantations. These large estates employ about 20% of the total paid workforce; the labor is largely unskilled and the wages are low.

CASH CROPS

Coffee, cocoa, and palm oil are the most important cash crops. Copra, the dried flesh of the coconut from which coconut oil is extracted, was a major contributor to the economy for many years, but a decline in the world commodity market made its production unrewarding. Since the country's independence in 1975, there has been a dramatic drop in copra output and the number of people employed on coconut plantations. Palm oil has replaced copra as the country's third biggest agricultural product, thanks to its high oil yield. Large oil palm plantations and processing plants are located in Oro, Milne Bay, and the western part of New Britain.

Although tea grown in the highlands is pleasant to drink, it has not met economic expectations, and cocoa is the second largest export crop after coffee. Rubber production is growing slowly, and tobacco is a cash crop that is produced for the domestic market.

The flesh and seeds of oil palm fruit yield a yellow oil used as edible fat and for making items such as soap and candles.

HIGH QUALITY HIGHLAND COFFEE

Coffee provides 20% of Papua New Guinea's exports. Most of it is cultivated in the five highland provinces of Simbu, Enga, Eastern Highlands, Western Highlands, and Southern Highlands. Up to 70% of the coffee is cultivated on small plots averaging slightly more than an acre (or half a hectare) in size, many of which are clan holdings. The mild Arabica bean that predominates is of a high quality and much in demand, and there are about 80 coffee-processing facilities that prepare the beans for local consumption and export. Coffee beans that are ready for picking resemble bright red berries. After picking, the berries are placed in a concrete trough where the fleshy part is left to rot. The outer coat of the seed is then dried and removed and the remaining beans are collected.

PAPUAN NATIONALS

THE PHYSICAL FEATURES OF PEOPLE IN PAPUA NEW GUINEA vary greatly in terms of skin coloring, facial structure, and even body size. Most people have mixed racial origins—Papuan, Melanesian, Micronesian, and Polynesian. Papuans and Melanesians, who make up 95% of the population, are believed to be related to the Ainoid line, people with a heavy brow line who are believed to be the ancestors of the Australian aborigine. Micronesians and Polynesians are related to the Mongoloid line and have more Asian features. The demarcation between the groups is indeterminate, and clan ties are more important than racial ones. It is common for a person to identify with a clan or tribal name—for example Motu or Duna. This conveys a strong sense of tribal cohesion, but not of national cohesion. On the basis of cultural and historical connections, regional groupings have developed as follows: New Guineans (northern mainland), Papuans (southern mainland), highlanders, and islanders.

Left: **The traditional protection in rainy weather is a large hood made from bark, bark cloth, or simply a large banana leaf held over the head.**

Opposite: **The child's light hair coloring is the result of a protein deficiency.**

49

POPULATION AND CHANGES

In 1996 the population was estimated to be 4.4 million; it is growing so quickly that it is expected to reach 5.7 million by the year 2010. This sudden rise reflects improved national health and the lack of a widespread use of birth control. The rapid increase is expected to put enormous pressure on health and education services, housing, and national resources.

The country has a young population with 41% under the age of 15 and 70% under the age of 29. The life expectancy remains low at 56.4 years for males and 58.1 years for females. The average birth rate is quite high, with an average of 4.4 births for each childbearing woman. The death rate stands at 10 deaths per 1,000 people; the world average is 9.9 per 1,000.

While development has brought improved medicine and modern technologies, it has also resulted in the erosion of a traditional lifestyle. People are no longer driven to observe taboos that formerly had a stabilizing effect, and gambling and excessive alcohol consumption have caused financial and social hardship among many. The challenge for today's population seems to be to discover what is truly valuable to them and to use these as guidelines to steer their lives.

WANTOK: FAMILY, CLAN, AND TRIBE

Family, clan, and tribe are the essential social units. Of these the extended family network is the most influential, and an intricate system of personal responsibilities and family obligations dictates the behavior of an individual in any given situation. A household may be called on to share its food, home, labor, land, or pigs with a family member or even someone from the same tribe, whether the relation is close or distant. This is the Melanesian custom of *wantok* ("WAN-tohk," or one talk) that acts as a social security network. A system of reciprocity means that something will usually be given in return—perhaps loyalty in a time of conflict, or help at a later date.

Property, a prerequisite of wealth, does not belong to the individual in the way that it does for Westerners. Ownership is vested in the household, of which there is usually a male head. In some instances property such as land and jewelry is owned by the whole clan or tribe and distributed according to a complex network of ties. Wealth is determined not just by having things in one's possession but also in the measure that one gives them away.

Above and opposite: **Out of economic necessity an increasing number of people are moving away from their tribes and into the modern way of living, becoming more focused on the individual than the clan.**

The village elders or "big men" are required to display their affluence by giving it away. This provides them with a great deal of influence because the villagers are then indebted to them. Big men do the heavy negotiating, settle disputes, and plan when to kill pigs. An elaborate system of negotiation, trading ceremonies, and ritualized battles exists between clans throughout the country to preserve or restore order.

Huli man in a distinctive wig made from human hair and held together with woven string. The women of the tribe do most of the work while the men concentrate on displaying their finery.

Black tigaso tree oil is traded all around the country in bamboo tubes. It is rubbed on the skin for an attractive dark sheen.

SELF-ADORNMENT

Western-style clothes are worn in the urban areas, particularly around Christian missions, and tend to be casual and geared towards the tropical climate. The women wear simple dresses, while the men wear shorts with a shirt (in the rural areas, the shirts are dispensable). Traditional clothing remains the norm for some tribes in the remote areas, and is especially relevant for special events.

The intimate relationship between the various clans and their surrounding environment is evident in the vibrant and ornate clothes they wear, both ceremonially and daily. Feathers, bones, leaves, seeds, shells, and natural pigments are the basis for dress. Often such finery is loaded with meaning; they represent the qualities of the wearer or the individual's status, or are symbolic representations of myths and customs revered by the tribe.

In Papua New Guinea, clothes consist less of fabrics and more of personal adornment; often it is a veritable work of art. The bright plumage of birds of paradise and other types of feathers are woven into elaborate headdresses for the men; these are then decorated with valuable shells and animal teeth. Several groups, such as the Huli and Komblo in the highlands, weave huge wigs from human hair and burrs, and decorate them with paints, dried flowers, and even iridescent beetles. The highlanders in particular favor nose piercing. The septum, the fleshy wall between the two nostrils, is pierced with a sharp piece of wood, bone or cassowary quill, and any variety of impressive objects are placed through the hole, including boar tusks, cassowary quills or bones, long dried grasses, or shells.

Loincloths or *laplaps* ("LAP-laps") tend to be more like aprons, with a longer section of cloth or strands of woven cords and leaves worn at the front, and a smaller bunch of leaves tucked into the waistband behind. Several tribes near the western border wear penis gourds and little else. The gourds are a long marrow-like fruit, up to three feet (0.9 meters) in length; these are dried, cut open and worn over the penis and tied to the waist with string. Cassowary bones, and other daggers and tools, are tucked into woven arm and leg bands. Sometimes ritual scar designs are cut into the flesh at a boy's coming of age, especially along the Sepik River where the designs represent the claw marks of crocodiles.

The painting of faces, bodies, and hair is practiced among both sexes, traditionally with charcoal and pigments, but modern paints are now favored for their brightness. Both men and women rub their skins with a variety of leaves and oils, including pig fat, to leave an attractive sheen.

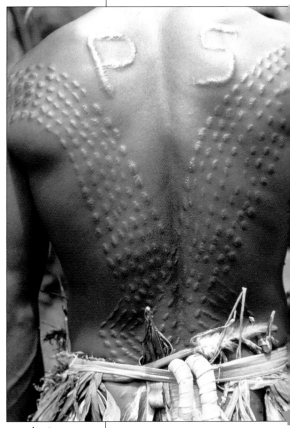

Ritual scar designs are cut into the flesh over the arms, shoulders, and upper body. Clay and ashes are rubbed into the cuts to ensure that they heal as raised keloid scars.

WOMEN'S DRESSING

Women's traditional dress is colorful but less elaborate than the men's. It is customary in some areas for women to wear tattoos on the face. The tattoos are made in a painful process, using just a needle and charcoal. Lines of dots in the shapes of suns and stars, curved parallel lines, and arrows decorate the face.

Women in most areas wear plain grass or other simple skirts and are usually barebreasted. In some regions unwed girls modestly cover themselves with a small woven patch of fabric, which is discarded when they marry. Strings of beads, leaves, feathers, and teeth are worn in abundance for ceremonial occasions.

While women wear headdresses for special events, these tend to be smaller and less ornate than those of the men. Huge woven bags called *bilums* ("BILL-uhms") are used to carry everything from babies to firewood, with the strap placed on the head and the weight of the load falling behind.

WOMEN IN MOURNING

Mourning women are required in several areas to wear numerous loops of grass seeds that range in color from pale gray to white. These are referred to in English as Job's Tears. A full load of these can weigh up to 31 pounds (14 kilograms). Each day the woman removes one loop. Mourning ends when she takes off the last loop of seeds, which is usually about nine months after the death of her husband. In some areas, the women coat themselves with a bluish-gray clay while in mourning.

In some parts of the country, the widow and other close female relatives of the dead man will have part of a finger removed from above the first joint as part of the funeral ritual. The finger-cutting ceremony is seen as a sign of grief and a sacrifice to placate the ancestral spirits. A male member of the tribe who performs the ritual knocks the grieving woman's elbow sharply on a stone to numb the arm before he uses a small stone adze to sever the finger at the joint. The remaining stump is wrapped in healing plants and the hand is bounded in a banana leaf.

Virtually all negotiations and village politics are conducted by the men. Nevertheless, a woman is sometimes forced by circumstances to take on a man's duties should he be away hunting or seeking paid employment away from the village.

POWERFUL TABOOS

Just as the men in a clan have their secret rituals, so do the women. There is knowledge which is never passed on to the men, involving magic and traditional medicine that only women can practice. The fear of being cursed by a witch holds many a brave hunter in its grip. There are powerful taboos relating to menstruation, the effects of which are so potent that in some tribes all women sleep in a separate dwelling from other villagers.

In certain places along the Sepik the women even have their own separate walking tracks in the village. In some areas the men cook their own food in the belief that any contact with women weakens them, and men protect themselves with herbs and magic before engaging in sexual relations with their wives. In the Sepik area, the men often while away the day lounging around in the cool shade of the men's houses, which the women are barred from entering.

LIFESTYLE

THE PEOPLE IN THE URBAN AND RURAL AREAS live vastly different lifestyles. The urban areas, with their Western-style housing, shopping, and conveniences, come with the comforts of modern living. The remote villages, on the other hand, rarely have electricity, unless cash cropping or mining have bought wealth and generators; they also lack proper roads and sanitary water supplies. Swarms of mosquitoes and sandflies fill the air near any swamp or river, and the smoke-filled interiors of houses are the only deterrent to these pests.

Only 15% of the population live in the urban centers, with the rest living in the rural areas. The government provides some funding for the building of low-cost housing, particularly in Port Moresby and Lae, but demand always exceeds production. As a result people construct small dwellings using an assortment of materials. These shelters are often clustered at the urban fringes and soon develop into shantytowns.

Left: **People are drawn to cities like Mt. Hagen in search of work and material gain, and the country is witnessing a growing cash economy.**

Opposite: **A villager hunts for the maggotlike grubs found inside the sago palm. Boiled grubs make a valuable source of protein in the diet.**

Many houses are constructed on stilts as protection against flooding and to facilitate defense in times of fighting; the stilts also position the houses above the height at which many mosquitoes and sandflies swarm.

VILLAGE LIFE

Outside the towns most housing is constructed using the resources found in the forests or swamps, with the occasional addition of industrial materials such as corrugated iron sheets. They vary from small huts at ground level, with a single room housing a single family, to large communal longhouses accommodating an extended family or segregated groups of men or women.

The houses are arranged in long rows or in circular clusters and may be rectangular or round in shape. The house frame is a strong wooden or bamboo structure, and is topped with thatched roofs of strong kunai grass, sago palm fronds, or other broad leaves. Wooden or bamboo slats or bark laced together with thin cane strips form walls; in some regions wooden panels are used.

A fire is usually left smoldering in a central hearth of dirt, stones, or a clay fire bowl. People like to sit around the fire mainly because the smoke helps to deter mosquitoes. After dark the fire is often the only source of light in villages with little or limited use of electricity or gas. The smoke escapes any way it can as windows are not necessarily desirable in a land infested with flying insects, drenched in monsoonal rains, and susceptible to tribal warfare. Inside the house there may be wooden beds, mats, or coarse fiber bedcovers. Food and other goods are commonly stored in baskets or string bags hung from the rafters, or in unglazed clay pots.

A village clearing is reserved for communal gatherings and it is the women's job to sweep it. Many highland villages have a wide ditch built around them to protect them against attacks and to prevent pigs, chickens, and small children from wandering out into the surrounding wilderness.

WEALTH IN SHELLS AND PIGS

Paper money and coins are relatively new in Papua New Guinea; paper money was once particularly mistrusted. As recently as 20 years ago, some people insisted on being paid only in coins. Even today many people set more value by traditional wealth than by the national currency. While an average pig may be worth around K300 to K400 (US$216–288), with a sow worth around K600 (US$432), most people would prefer to own the pig itself instead of the cash. Likewise, cassowaries and any weapons or jewelry made from parts of this animal are highly sought after.

Currency still in use includes kina shells. Like the kina shell after which it is named, the one-kina coin has a hole in the middle so that it can be strung and worn around the neck.

The national currency is named after the kina shell, a large crescent shape cut from the gold-lipped pearl shell. Kina shells are worn proudly on a length of string threaded between two holes in the shell and are still used in trade and barter. Occasionally, an individual shell will be given its own name, and the number of knots in its string are an indication of the number of owners the shell has had. In the highlands it is common to see long necklaces made of tiny bamboo sticks strung in a ladderlike fashion. Each strip on these *omak* ("OH-mak") necklaces represents either 10 pigs or 10 kina shells given away or lent by the owner and are an important guide to the wearer's status.

Trade is commonly conducted with nonpaper money. In Milne Bay, business can be conducted with grass skirts (valued around K5 to K10; US$3.60–7.20) or dry bundles of etched banana leaves called *doba* ("DOH-bah"). In New Britain, *tambu* ("TAHM-boo"), or tiny shells strung on a piece of bamboo worth about K0.10 (7 cents) per dozen, are used as currency, especially in the markets.

A Japanese-made mini-truck serving as a PMV, or "public motor vehicle." Each PMV has a government-employed driver and a conductor who finds out where one intends to disembark and collects the fare midway through the trip.

MOVING AROUND

The fastest and easiest way to travel in Papua New Guinea is by air. Much of the country's development has depended on its aviation facilities, and most mineral and forestry exploration takes place with sophisticated equipment transported by air. However, many of the airstrips are small and rough, and flights often have long waiting lists.

Along the waterways, especially the Sepik River, the dugout canoe is king. The traffic can get quite heavy on the river on market days. Large- and medium-sized freighters and passenger boats provide transportation between the islands, but it may take a couple of days to reach a destination because freight is loaded on or taken off along the way. Villagers make use of their own boats ranging from traditional canoes, diesel-run wooden boats, or small dinghies with outboard motors known as "speedies" or "banana boats."

The majority of roads are rough, and travelers can be ambushed by armed robbers. Sometimes heavy rainfall converts roads into impassable muddy bogs. Nevertheless, they are useful for shorter journeys and for those with little money. One can choose to walk, the road often being the only clearing through dense vegetation, or take a PMV. These "public motor vehicles" can be any vehicle from a truck with hard benches to a Japanese-made minibus. They travel along predetermined routes through the towns and countryside. Despite a lack of policing of the roads in the rural areas, the PMVs are quite safe to travel in because the drivers are aware of the stiff payback fines should they run over even a chicken, let alone if they injured a pedestrian or passenger.

LAND TENURE

About 97% of land in Papua New Guinea comes under traditional land ownership laws, a stark contrast to the Western system based on individual ownership backed by legal documents. Traditional ownership is based on human memory, often held by a community, and distributed according to a complex web of individual and clan rights. The systems differ from place to place. Disputes between tribes over land ownership boundaries are a historical cause of warfare, and tensions still run high today between different tribal groups and clans within any single tribe.

Some areas remain communally owned. This becomes a problem when land transfer is required for nontraditional purposes—for example the sale of land for cash cropping, or the establishment of mining rights in a particular area. Different groups may stake their claim on a single piece of land based on each group's oral history, and disputes inevitably arise. Sometimes the wrong group of people is paid compensation for the use of the land.

Some government road and electricity projects as well as proposed mining developments may cross several traditional boundaries. A situation then arises in which too many groups claim compensation and the project has to be abandoned because of mounting costs.

Payback must be made for deaths incurred in battle. If a village is unable to make the payment immediately, a truce is declared for the duration of the payback term, which can last for months or even years.

PAYBACK AND WARFARE

In Papua New Guinea, everything is owned by someone. Even seemingly remote areas of land have a traditional owner somewhere, and ownership of individual animals is known throughout the entire village. Should land be used, the owners expect immediate and generous compensation or rent. Any damage (whether intended or accidental) caused to life, limb, or property requires ritual compensation to avert similar violence in return.

The sizes of tribes vary from a few hundred to a few thousand members, and different tribes have traditionally been hostile toward each other. Each tribe or clan is collectively held responsible for the actions of its individual members and actively seeks compensation if one of its own members becomes a victim. Failing to make the appropriate payback compensation is a worse crime than the original act, and revenge is accordingly brutal. Pigs are the favored payback currency, although other goods such as kina shells, trade-store food, cash, and even cartons of beer are acceptable. Tribal war may result should negotiations fail.

BRIDE PRICE AS MARRIAGE CONTRACT

Marriage is less about the individual's ties and more about the wider social relationships that are strengthened through the marriage contract. An essential element is the payment of a "bride price" by the groom to his wife's parents or clan.

The traditional marriage ceremony centers around the final payment of the bride price. The groom and his clan, dressed in their customary finery, walk to the ceremonial clearing where the goods are laid out in front of the bride's clan. Leaf-wrapped kina shells rubbed with red ocher, pigs, cash notes attached to a large display pole, and even cassowaries can form part of this important payment. They are examined by the bride's family and the marriage is sealed once the goods are accepted.

These payments are still common even in the cities where marriages take place between members of clans from different provinces, and among Christians too, with the addition of a church ceremony. Despite efforts by village councils to control the prices, payments can be high. In the highlands, it can consist of 20 pigs and K200 (US$144) or more in cash; in the cities, an average of K12,000 ($8,640) changes hands, and the sum can rise even higher among wealthy families.

In the Mendi region, brides are dressed in black for their weddings and are required to wear this for an entire month afterward. They darken their skin with soot and tigaso oil, which is also black.

Traditionally, adultery is considered a crime worse than murder. It is considered an insult to the aggrieved spouse's entire clan and may be punishable by death. Today this strict code has been relaxed, but adultery is still a very serious offense in some groups.

Childbirth is a risk. The infant mortality rate is high and in some areas a child is never named in the first six to 12 months because it is believed that if it dies with a given name, its spirit would need attention. Maternal mortality is high too, with as many as 20 maternal deaths for every 1,000 births.

THE ROLE OF WOMEN

Women are traditionally considered subordinate to men, although there are a few exceptions. In a few societies in the New Guinea islands and Milne Bay, property is passed on matrilineally—that is, men inherit property through the female line; for example, a man may inherit goods from his mother's brother. After all, women in these societies perform the bulk of subsistence farming, tend pigs, raise children, and prepare food.

Nevertheless, the women are not accorded social or political equality. The men are still custodians of family property, wield power in decision-making, and receive the cash and the choicest cuts of food. The women have little recourse should they disagree with their husbands, fathers, or elders. Many men feel justified in beating their wives or daughters. While this is illegal, the law fails to protect women because it is virtually impossible to police such cases, especially in the remote areas.

There are instances when the women band together to form women's groups and collectives. They have also set up their own trading networks, shareholding concerns, and educational support systems, achieving successes and reaping monetary and social benefits. Some women have risen above the obstacles placed before them to reach management level in both private and public sectors, or respected positions in their home communities.

Paid employment would appear to be the surest way to leave behind the traditional requirement of subservience, as it allows the women to participate in a modern world. The difficulty is that many rural societies

When the country gained its independence, the government named as one of its goals "a rapid increase in the equal and active participation of women in all forms of economic and social activity."

still hold negative perceptions about sending their daughters through school. The labor a girl provides in tending to her domestic chores is greater than that of her brother, so in times of economic shortage a girl will be taken out of school before her brother.

Men often consider a woman's value as they would a commodity. Since the women are responsible for agricultural production, having a wife is a requirement for creating wealth. In some areas the amount of land allotted to a man's family for farming depends on the number of women he has in the household, and polygamy is practiced in many areas to maximize wealth and status. The more wives a man has, the more pigs they can rear for him. Big men in particular have several wives who are regarded as a symbol of prestige. Daughters who are married earn their parents a bride payment that can be quite substantial, and the temptation can be to go for the union that is the most profitable or politically beneficial to the parents.

A female cashier serves a customer at a Western-style supermarket.

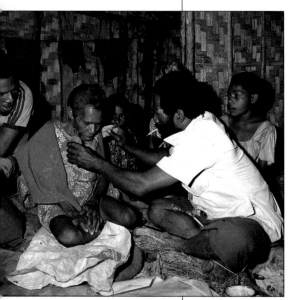

A sick woman being attended to by a village healer.

HEALTH CARE

The health system is continually under pressure as the population grows, and life expectancy figures are still low. The delivery of health services rests on a system of first-aid posts (one post for every 5,000 people) staffed by orderlies with rudimentary medical knowledge and hygiene skills. Health centers which cater for around 12,000 people each have a higher level of expertise. Finally, there are a series of provincial hospitals with trained medical staff; the ratio is one doctor to every 12,000 people. The Christian churches employ 16% of all health workers, run several hospitals, and provide the most thorough training for nurses. In many areas people still administer their own healing methods, ranging from medicinal plants to a belief in the healing power of body paint.

Malaria is endemic in Papua New Guinea and it also contributes to the high infant mortality rate. Widescale mobile vaccination programs have done much to halt the spread of infectious diseases such as tuberculosis and yaws, a highly contagious skin disease. However, the fight is never over in a country where climate and remoteness hamper large-scale health improvements.

Malnutrition is a factor in many deaths; often simple illnesses do not respond well to treatment because of a weakened immune system. About 10% of the population have access to safe drinking water, but many people do not understand the link between poor sanitation and disease, and diarrheal diseases continue to take their toll. Education about hygiene and nutrition is fundamental to improve the standard of health in all the regions.

EDUCATION

The national literacy rate has improved rapidly, with 72.2% of the population aged 15 years and over able to read. When Papua New Guinea gained its independence, the government expressed two goals concerning education: universal education at the primary level and access to education for as many as possible.

The first six years of education, starting at the age of 7, are compulsory, with classes held in government-provided, community-based schools. In remote areas, these schools are sometimes little more than open-air, palm-thatched structures, and having them around does not guarantee enrollment. Most instruction takes place in English and some in Pidgin, although some provincial governments are experimenting with the teaching of literacy in the local language.

For higher education, there is the University of Papua New Guinea in Port Moresby and the University of Technology in Lae, along with colleges of higher education in most provinces.

A teachers' training college in Goroka teaches silk screening as a craft in addition to the usual academic learning.

RELIGION

THERE SEEM TO BE AS MANY DIVERGENT BELIEF SYSTEMS in Papua New Guinea as there are tribes with different languages. Communities isolated from each other have, over thousands of years, passed on their myths and rituals, most of them based on people's close contact with their surrounding landscape. The presence of the forest or a river is keenly felt and respected, for although they give sustenance, they can also be cruel adversaries to human existence.

Two elements are common in traditional beliefs: the practice of magic and belief in a spirit world. Spirits are regarded as belonging to the recently dead and to the ancestors, and it is believed that there are also other types of spirits that inhabit the natural world.

Christianity is the professed religion of 90% of Papuan nationals. There is also a small but active Muslim community in Papua New Guinea.

Spirits may be malevolent and therefore require placating. Less malevolent spirits are sometimes courted, and important ventures are never started without first seeking the spirits' approval and intervention.

Left: **Many traditional beliefs revolve around superstition and fear of the unknown.**

Opposite: **Roman Catholic mission at Mt. Wilhelm.**

A Christian baptism by water immersion in a lake.

CHRISTIAN CHURCHES

Christianity was introduced early in the country's history during contact between the local people and the outside world. Missions were set up throughout the country by Christians who spent decades of their lives living close to and working with the local people. The influence of the various churches has been such that by 1960, Papua New Guinea had become a predominantly Christian country. Even today Christian churches continue to run and fund hospitals, plantations, and schools.

Although approximately 90% of the population identify themselves as Christians, many may not participate in church activities on a regular basis. The major Christian churches and organizations that are represented are the Lutherans, Baptists, Seventh Day Adventists, Roman Catholics, Anglicans, United Church, Jehovah's Witnesses, and the Salvation Army. Many who profess a belief in Christianity practice clan rituals alongside their churchgoing without any apparent conflict of ideals.

CANNIBALISM

Papua New Guinea's laws support the right of the individual to practice his or her beliefs freely, provided they do not infringe on the general principles of humanity. One practice that was outlawed nearly as soon as it was discovered by the colonial government was cannibalism. Cannibalism, or the eating of human flesh, has been practiced for centuries by groups such as the Hewa and the Fore. It is not about murder, but rather eating the flesh of one's own clan people who have died through natural causes or disease, either in the belief that it protects one from illness, or to release the spirit of the deceased from the body. These groups believe that a spirit that is not released is doomed to spend its days in a sort of limbo.

The body is prepared and cooked by a strict code, then divided among clan members according to each individual's relationship to the deceased. At one time it was considered an honor to partake in this practice. Hostility toward the *guvmen* ("GUV-men," or government) who declared this practice illegal caused the Hewa region in the southern highlands to be closed to outsiders until 1965.

Some headhunting tribes had the custom of bleaching the skulls of their victims and putting them on display in their villages as trophies.

FATAL LAUGHING DISEASE

Cannibalistic feasting seems to have resulted in the transmission of disease rather than its prevention. *Kuru* ("KOO-roo") is the name given to an agonizing and fatal "laughing disease" that affects the central nervous system. More women than men have contracted this disease, probably because the men are greatly restricted by taboos concerning the body parts they may consume.

The link between this disease and cannibalistic practices was discovered by a Christian mission. However, the people themselves continued to attribute the disease to sorcery and remained unconvinced for a long time that the tradition was harmful. It is believed that cannibalism is no longer practiced, and while a few people continue to fall ill with *kuru*, it is thought to be the result of the long incubation period of the disease.

Above: **Roof of a spirit house in the Sepik region.**

Opposite: **Huli medicine man posing with the skulls of his ancestors.**

PLACES OF WORSHIP

Christian churches and mission houses are present throughout Papua New Guinea and vary widely in design and complexity. Urban centers tend to have larger churches constructed in a modern Western manner, while in rural areas they can be simple halls made from whatever local materials are available.

Outside the influence of Christianity, traditional beliefs are still being followed. Along the Sepik are soaring *haus tamborans* ("house TAM-bor-ans"), or spirit houses in which are stored items of cultural and religious significance. They are made from materials similar to those used in the local houses, but have high prow-like facades. These have decorative panels carved and painted with masklike ancestor faces, or representations of spirit animals or totems. Initiated men are the only ones permitted to enter these houses, and it is believed that a breach of this taboo can result in death to the offender. Fertility rites, magical ceremonies, and male initiation take place here.

The other most important religious space is the clearing in the village, where all types of dances, singing, and communal rituals take place. The rituals enact traditional stories and beliefs, prepare for important events, or are an attempt to bring about a desired outcome. Taboos and tradition dictate the exact formula of these rituals, down to costume and body paint used, the words sung, the music played, the people who participate, and even the food consumed.

MAGIC AND SORCERY

A feature of Melanesian society is widespread belief in magic, practiced by ordinary people for beneficial reasons (to aid healing, for example) and by sorcerers who wield it for power. When practiced by the people, magic is observed in superstitions and daily rituals, and permeates all areas of village life. The magic of sorcerers, on the other hand, is veiled in secrecy and fear, and disease and misfortune are attributed to the workings of enemy sorcerers. In some societies women use men's fear of their witchcraft to manipulate them.

Magic is practiced daily to ensure successful harvests, gain victory against a warring tribe, or find a suitable mate. Plants are cultivated or gathered for these purposes, some as medicine, accompanied by rituals and spells.

Some tribes seek revenge against those who have wronged them by bringing illness on their enemies. Sometimes magic is invoked to cast illness on a whole clan or tribe. At other times, the sorcerer seeks to replace an individual victim's spirit with a stone, causing the person to die. It is also believed that sickness can be inflicted by collecting a victim's personal items and knotting them in a special way; burning the whole parcel results in death.

A bird mask represents the people's belief in the spirit world.

SPIRIT ANIMALS

The most important spirits are usually those of the ancestors, but in some areas non-human spirits feature more prominently. These may be perceived in animal or monster forms; for example people living near the Sepik fear the *masalai* ("mass-ah-LAY," or crocodile), and offerings of *buai* ("BWAI," or betel nut) are thrown into treacherous rapids inhabited by them. Such spirits are regarded to have individual personalities and be able to communicate their anger or goodwill. The people take much care to please the spirits, believing that they can affect the fortune of an individual or tribe, and this forms an integral part of ritualistic beliefs and practices.

Birds play a significant role in these traditions. Each Dani clan has ties with a particular bird species, thought to be clan members. To the Enga, different bird species are inhabited by ghosts, and hearing their call requires certain behavior to avert personal disaster. For example, the cry of the small tinalupi bird requires the hearer to sacrifice possums or pigs, or sickness and even death will result. In their desperation, people have been known to chop off their fingers or other body parts in an attempt to placate ghosts that they believe are attacking them.

Not all spirit animals are considered evil. Some spirits are thought to bring about bountiful crops, successful hunting, and personal achievement. These beliefs are slowly dying as Christianity spreads, education reaches more people, and the skeptical ways of the modern world begin to influence their attitudes.

SONG, DANCE, AND FIRESIDE STORIES

Singing and dancing are not only an outlet for entertainment, but also an important method for handing down oral histories through succeeding generations. They provide a valuable means of committing information to the communal memory in the absence of written records. New songs are composed for current and important events, such as initiations and funerals, and to commemorate victories.

These songs and dances are not only sung or performed at festivals and ceremonies, but are a part of daily life. During the planting of crops or the construction of houses, for example, both the men and women sing, either by themselves or in unison. A single voice sometimes rings out down the green hillside, followed by the response of chanting voices of all ages from nearby areas.

At the fireside the singing and dancing continues, this time accompanied by storytelling. The storyteller is treated with great respect, and many tales deal with the existence of good and evil, the origin of special foods, family ties, warfare, the beginning of humankind, how people came to inhabit their special region, or the origin of their tribe or clan. Often the dividing line between magic, religious beliefs, clan histories, and social ceremonies is difficult to distinguish. Many of the people's festivals and art are an expression of their religious beliefs.

Sorcery: the need to placate the spirits of the ancestors, and the fear of evil influences are common themes in the people's stories.

CREATION STORY

One story tells of a being that created humanity by drawing people in the sand, then pouring blood over them. The Mangen and Mamusi highlanders ascribe creation to Nutu, who created humans and placed their soul, or *kanu* ("KAH-noo"), inside their liver, or *lona* ("LOH-na"). In death, the *kanu* flies back to Nutu, who is the master of all things.

MATHS Revision:

1 50% /
2 75% /
3 36½% ✗ /

   2 mins /
   125 /
   None of them /
12 568 /
13 100 /
14 ½, ⅓, ¾, $\frac{3}{6}$, ⅛ /
15 30 eggs /
16 32 km /
17 K66.31^t left /
18 12 /
19 1.26 pm //
20 54 cm^2

19/20 Good.

LANGUAGE

OVER 700 LANGUAGES AND DIALECTS are spoken in Papua New Guinea. Some are spoken by only a few hundred people in a community, and neighboring villages only 6 miles (10 km) apart may have completely different languages. Engan, the indigenous language with the largest number of speakers, is spoken by only about 20,000 people. While some of these languages are interrelated and share common dialects, many are radically different in origin. They are generally classified as either Austronesian or non-Austronesian.

Austronesian languages are related to tongues spoken in Indonesia, the Philippines, and other regions of the Pacific. Motu, spoken in the Port Moresby area, is an Austronesian language. The non-Austronesian languages, which are believed to be older, include those spoken in the highlands and in small areas on Bougainville, New Ireland, and New Britain. They defy simple classification.

Left: **An Australian teacher encourages a deaf girl to feel the sound of her voice by touching her vocal chords. The girl learns by imitating the throat movement.**

Opposite: Learning simple mathematics, although the people's traditional concepts are limited and different from the Western model.

Above: **A group of villagers are fascinated by the workings of a tape recorder, never having seen one before.**

Opposite: **Bibles and other books being displayed on board a visiting ship.**

ENGLISH AS THE OFFICIAL LANGUAGE

When the country came under Australian governance, English was used in administration and education; it was subsequently adopted as the official language of Papua New Guinea because of its commercial utility. Today it is the language of government, education, commerce, and higher levels of administration but is not yet spoken on a national scale. For now it is spoken by only a small percentage of the population who have access to education.

The government would like to see English used more widely, because teaching children in Pidgin means that a large number of school and technical books would have to be translated from English. Besides, if Pidgin were to become the official national language, people would be using a means of verbal and written communication that is not easily understood or used elsewhere in the world, and dealings with outsiders would be difficult.

MELANESIAN PIDGIN

Hiri Motu, a language developed by the Motu for their trading expeditions in the Gulf of Papua and thus used outside its original borders, was adapted by the Armed Native Constabulary to become Police Motu in British New Guinea. It became a sort of lingua franca for people in the region until the introduction of English.

Difficulties in communication remained, however, and in the absence of a common language one needed to be found that would be easy for speakers of many tongues to adopt. Hence Pidgin, or *Tok Pisin* ("TOHK pee-sin"), developed to fill the gap.

Pidgin is a mixture of English, German, and Melanesian words set to a Malay grammar pattern that is uncomplicated and easy to pick up. The language arose among the Melanesian people who were hired as plantation labor in Australia and the Pacific. Other regions of the Pacific have their own local patterns of Pidgin.

The Pidgin spoken in Papua New Guinea is sometimes called Neo-Melanesian, but is more commonly known as Papua New Guinean Pidgin. As it originated around Rabaul, the Melanesian contribution is strongly flavored by the language patterns around the eastern part of New Britain.

It is not customary to ask a person's name upon meeting, and even people who know each other's names do not ordinarily use them. Like all customs, however, this is slowly changing in the urban centers.

Some of the words, especially the verbs, have a strong German origin, but *Tok Pisin* is based heavily on English, and this influence is increasingly felt. For example, a towel used to be called *laplap bilong waswas* ("LAP-lap BEE-long WAS-was," or cloth for washing), but is now referred to simply as *taul* ("TAH-ol"). Other words from geographically close languages have crept in, for example from Indonesian, and many modern Australian colloquialisms have been integrated into the main body of vocabulary and make for colorful speech. *Naiswan* ("NAIS-wan") comes from the Australian "nice one" and is used, as in Australia, to express congratulations or approval.

Over time, there have been criticisms of the language as if it were merely a crude, patronizing, and inferior version of English. In reality, it is a highly effective language that is living and growing and has evolved some of its own features. Its success is determined by the ease and enthusiasm with which the nation has adopted it, and it has largely replaced Motu, which was the former lingua franca around the southern Papua area.

One of the features of *Tok Pisin* is its limited vocabulary. It has around 1,300 words that do the equivalent work of 6,000 words in English. This leads to ingenious combinations of words strung together to provide the clearest meaning. Take the body parts, for example. Instead of a single word for toe, *Tok Pisin* uses *pinga bilong lek* ("PIN-gah BEE-long LEK," or finger belonging to the leg), and the elbow is called *skru bilong han* ("SKROO BEE-long HAN," or screw belonging to the hand). While *kaikai*

("KHAI-khai") means food, breakfast is *kaikai bilong moning* ("KHAI-khai BEE-long MOH-ning"), lunch is *kaikai bilong belo* ("KHAI-khai BEE-long BEH-loh"), and dinner is *kaikai bilong apinun* ("KHAI-khai BEE-long AP-ee-noon"). Belo means bell but *belo kaikai* means food bell, signifying noon. Therefore *kaikai bilong belo* means food for noon, or lunch. Lunch is also known as *liklik kaikai* ("LIK-lik KHAI-khai"), or little food, or even just *belo*. Dessert is sweet *kai*. Anything can thus be described by this process of circumlocution.

Despite the success of Pidgin and Motu in providing common languages, and the increasing numbers of children who are learning English in school, not everyone knows these languages. When this happens people rely heavily on body language and action, as well as a smattering of common words, to get the message across.

A signboard in Pidgin outside a bar operating in the Ok Tedi mining community stating the house rules for customers.

COUNTING IN TOK PISIN

Cardinal numbers from one to 10 are: *wan, tu, tri, foa, faiv, siks, seven, et, nain, ten*, with pronunciation based on the English phonetic interpretation of the spelling. One hundred is *wan handet* ("HAN-dett") and 1,000 is *wan tausen* ("TAU-ssen").

When referring to amounts of money, the time, and mathematics, the word denoting the root number is used—for example, *nain kina* ("NAIN KEE-nah," or nine kina). When describing a number of anything else, the suffix *pela* ("PEH-lah") is used—for example, *wanpela pikinini* ("WAN-PEH-LA PEE-kee-nin-ee") means one child, and *tripela meri* ("TREE-PEH-LAH MEH-ree") means three women. To describe ordinal numbers such as first, second, and third, the word *namba* ("NAM-bah") is placed before the cardinal number as in *namba wan* ("NAM-bah WAN") for first, *namba tu* ("NAM-bah TOO") for second, and so on.

Opposite: **This radio station in Goroka may not have the most modern equipment but it broadcasts news, music, and regional announcements in English, Pidgin, and the regional languages.**

COUNTING THE PAPUAN WAY

Westerners take their almost universal decimal system for granted. In Papua New Guinea there are probably more than 50 traditional methods of counting, devised by individual groups for their own uses. The decimal method, based on units grouped into tens, has caused outright bafflement in some areas, and modern mathematical concepts are not easily grasped by people whose traditional systems are different. In some areas no words exist beyond the first few numbers; any number greater than two or three becomes "some" and beyond that is "many."

Whereas most worldwide mathematical systems count with a base of 10, some groups in Papua New Guinea have a base of only two. After counting one and two, there is no three, so it is back to one again. One group has done a little better. It has a counting base of 47 made up of 23 points on the right side of the body (consisting of fingers, toes, and joints) and another 23 on the left. The nose is the 47th point, after which the counting starts at one again.

Considerable confusion has arisen, especially in trade stores, because the rural owners did not understand the percentage mark-up system based on a decimal concept and failed to charge a profit margin on their goods. Fortunately the use of simple pocket calculators accompanied by a few demonstrations has solved the problem.

TELEVISION AND RADIO

Radio has been around for some time, and it is the principal medium for mass broadcasting in a country where information has traditionally been passed on orally. The National Broadcasting Commission was set up in 1973, and it operates a national AM and FM radio station out of Port Moresby (largely in English), along with provincial services in Pidgin, Motu, and other regional languages. Most of the nation is able to receive these broadcasts, and they contain regional and national news, community information announcements, religious programs, current affairs, sports reporting, entertainment, and local music.

Papua New Guinea did not have its own television station until 1987, when broadcasting stations were established in Port Moresby, Lae, and other centers. Papua New Guinea has only one television station, but most people tune in to QTV from North Queensland in Australia, and with the help of a satellite dish pick up Indonesian and Malaysian programs along with CNN. Videos are also popular, and they are available from trade stores, hotels, and *kai* shops (food stores). Despite television's popularity, television sets are still reasonably rare with one television set for every 367 people.

POST AND TELECOMMUNICATION SYSTEMS

Papua New Guinea has had a postal system since 1886 when the *SS Victory* carried mail between Australia and New Guinea, mostly using an Australian stamp system. Papua and New Guinea issued their first stamp in 1952, and today Papua New Guinea's stamps feature largely traditional themes. An extensive postal system is in operation, but mail is not delivered to individual homes. Instead, post offices and regional post agencies (set up in trade stores, for example) provide collection from private post boxes and mail bags, and over the counter as well. Domestic mail is carried by air, sea, and road, and air mail carried within the country does not incur any extra fee. Delivery to remote areas is carried out by air, along with the transportation of people and supplies.

The country's urban centers have a fully automated telephone system, while in the remote areas connections are powered by solar energy. The radio phone is operator-connected to very remote areas. There are no area codes, with direct dialing between centers.

FAXES AND THE INTERNET

As an alternative to the mail or telephone service, there is always the *kwik piksa leta* ("KWIK PIK-sa LET-tah," meaning quick picture letter or fax) that has become very popular. Many businesses have them, and the public can send faxes from post offices for several kina. They can be a cheap alternative to long-distance phone calls, and fax numbers are listed in the directory along with the phone numbers.

The Internet is another medium that has been adopted by some individuals to access written information, although public access to the service is minimal. There are a number of sites providing fact files about Papua New Guinea, as well as chat sites for the South Pacific in Pidgin (not necessarily Melanesian Pidgin, but mutually understandable).

Stacks of newspaper waiting to be recycled.

NEWSPAPERS AND BOOKS

The country has a single daily newspaper, the Australian-owned, English-language *Post Courier*, with a daily circulation of 41,000. It is the most widely circulated daily in the South Pacific, delivered to regional centers by air. The weekly *Wantok* is published in Pidgin by Word Publishing, set up by the Catholic, Anglican, Lutheran, and United churches. Word Publishing also has the English-language *The Times of Papua New Guinea* and the *New Nation*. The government Office of Information publishes a paper twice monthly in English, Motu, and Pidgin. It is designed for people with limited reading skills and is widely circulated through the rural areas.

Reading is steadily becoming popular as more people learn to read and proceed to higher levels of education. The availability of books is fair in the regional centers where bookshops, libraries, and schools are situated, but poor elsewhere. Many bookshops are Christian-based, but along with religious publications there is a wide range of books in Pidgin and English.

Stacks of newspaper waiting to be recycled.

ARTS

PAPUA NEW GUINEA'S ART FORMS are largely traditional and practiced in the course of daily living. In a climate where heat and moisture cause organic materials to decay rapidly, the emphasis is rarely on creating permanence. Much art is created with the process being as important as the final product so that, in some instances, it is not even displayed, or displayed briefly before being washed away (as with body painting), or stored out of sight (as in art created as part of a ritual). The art expressed by the people is therefore vibrant and often not labeled as art by its creators. It is closely entwined with religion, the songs and dances performed in festivals, and body adornment.

Above: **Tree bark cloth is made by beating sheets of bark between two large, rounded rocks until the bark thins and spreads out, and becomes more supple. In some areas men and women wear clothes made of the cloth. In other areas it is used much as a Western artist would use a piece of canvas.**

Opposite: **A Sepik mask distinguished by its elongated design. Such masks are generally made of wood, decorated with clay, and embedded with shell, hair, and pig's teeth. There is an almost African look about them.**

In modern Papua New Guinea, an effort is being made to collect and catalog the richness of the nation's art works, and the National Museum and Art Gallery is in charge of administering the National Cultural (Preservation) Act. Artifacts more than 20 years old are not permitted to leave the country unless they are being sent to overseas museums that already have good examples in their collections. The museum also advises people against selling their old cultural pieces to artifact buyers, and anyone who wishes to export such artifacts must obtain the permission of the museum.

The Institute of Papua New Guinea Studies conducts ongoing research into all facets of traditional culture. It makes archival recordings of traditional music, folklore, myths, and poetry, and films local arts and crafts. The institute encourages the development of new works in the contemporary setting and is a major publisher of modern poetry, novels, play scripts, and discussion papers. The National School of Arts provides training in traditional and contemporary art at the university level.

Above: **The rhythmic beat of** *kundu* **drums accompanies ritual dance and chanting.**

Opposite: **A Huli tribesman playing a sacred flute.**

TRADITIONAL MUSIC

Singing, chanting, and dancing are an integral part of a villager's daily life, a part of religious ritual, and an essential component in every festival. Various musical instruments accompany the singing and dancing, both in religious and secular applications. Drums are the main musical instruments used. Rhythmic drumming resounds at all celebrations and the drums are art works in themselves. The *kundu* ("KUHN-doo"), seen on the national coat of arms, is a small drum carved from a hollow wooden cylinder, narrow in the middle and wider at each end, resembling an hourglass. It is played with one hand. Lizard or snake skin is stretched over one end of the drum. It often has a handle and may have seeds, feathers, or other ornamentation. The *garamut* ("ga-rah-MUTT") drums, found along the Sepik, are larger and are made from a hollowed-out tree trunk.

Wind instruments are common throughout the country, varying widely in construction and the sounds produced. In one area of the Sepik, a series of eight long conical horns are played in a ritual, each with a different plaintive honking note being sounded by its player at the correct moment to create the hypnotic tune. In the highlands pottery flutes such as the ocarina, a globular clay flute, are made. Sacred flutes that are made in male and female pairs and are never played separately are usually saved for initiation rites. There is also a small nose flute played with the nose, and other flutes are made in various parts of the country from reeds or bamboo.

Horns and shells are sounded around the country; in some coastal areas they are used to signal warnings or other messages up and down the coast. Bullroarers are swung around on a length of cord and make a loud but eerie resonant moaning hum. New Britain has a musical bow made from a strip of palm with a string of vine, and the highlands have created a small harplike instrument. The *lanaut* ("LAH-nowt") from New Ireland is played for its range of animal and bird sounds.

Since the 1970s music and the arts have been an arena in which Papuans have struggled to reconcile the clash between traditional culture and the rapid onslaught of new ways. The government encourages the continuation and, in some cases, the revival of activities associated with traditional culture.

Most of the country's pop music is recorded in Rabaul, in the East New Britain province, which has at least two recording studios.

CONTEMPORARY MUSIC AND THEATER

Performing traditional songs and dances comes naturally to all Papuans. Doing so on a modern stage, with the technicalities of sound, lighting, and script is, however, a new medium for the people. In the 1970s and 1980s both the National Theater Company and the Raun Raun Theater took up the challenge.

The National Theater performs locally written plays and incorporates elements of traditional song, dance, and plays in its repertoire of puppet shows, dance productions, and folk and contemporary plays. Audiences include urban and rural people although the company has also performed in international arts festivals, where it has been well received. Community participation is encouraged through workshops that teach traditional dances, theater skills, and techniques.

The Raun Raun Theater, based in Goroka, aims to bring theater to several provinces—especially large villages whose residents would not ordinarily travel to the urban centers—and its mobile nature has allowed it to accommodate the special needs of the country. It has created its own theater school.

Both the National and Raun Raun theaters invite scripts by local people and incorporate uniquely Papuan perspectives in these productions so

SPECIAL SOUNDS

The people of Papua New Guinea can create extraordinary sounds by using their voices. Inspired largely by the forest, many groups have a characteristic sound, either as a warning or for celebration, that is picked up and repeated so that it resounds throughout the area. In the Sepik, various froglike noises are produced.

that they are culturally meaningful to their participants. Even though this type of theater is new to Papuan audiences, people relate easily to the theatrical medium because storytelling in oratory, music, and dance has always been a feature of their lives.

Music students at the National School of Arts are required to study both Western and Melanesian musical instruments, and many have chosen to create a synthesis between the two. The Sanguma rock band is one of the first to succeed with a homegrown style. It wrote songs in *Tok Pisin* and other local languages and blended traditional instruments and rhythms with contemporary Western ones. It was very popular both at home and with international audiences, paving the way for other popular Papuan bands. In Port Moresby, private clubs play modern jazz or blues music, and there are discotheques in the larger towns.

A member of the Sanguma rock band performing at an open-air concert in Port Moresby. The band's special brand of music mixes modern Western instruments with traditional ones.

A wood carver examines his completed work.

CARVINGS AND PAINTINGS

Apart from spectacular and colorful body embellishment, the visual arts are practiced by some groups of Papuans in their carvings and painting, using a variety of materials. The Hewa people from the Southern Highlands province make ocher paintings on flat sheets of bark; these are created to gain power over the ideas or animals represented on them, particularly before hunting. They are not displayed as decoration, but stored in small thatched shelters until they deteriorate.

Other regions have their own story boards traditionally carved from fragile bark; today these are constructed in a more sturdy manner, depicting in raised relief various village events. In the Gulf province, *gope* ("GOH-peh") or *hohao* ("HOH-how") boards are beautiful shield-shaped carvings thought to contain the spirits of ancestors, or heroes and guardians of the village. They are traditionally kept in the men's houses, but today have lost some of their spiritual significance. They were traditionally carved with stone axes from the old wood of canoes, with cassowary bones and shark's

ART TABOOS

The production of carvings and paintings has traditionally been enshrouded by a number of taboos. These are observed to ensure that the relevant spirit can inhabit the carving or sacred object. Abstinence from certain foods or fasting may be required, and the carver generally cannot associate with women as they may have an adverse effect on the performance of secret rituals and magic. The artist is highly respected for his role, both religious and as a recorder of myths and special events. Today much of the religious significance of art has been lost, and the carver or painter may have other reasons for his work, especially that of trading for income.

teeth used for the finer details. They are colored with paints made from burnt shells (white), charcoal (black), and clays (reds and browns). Similar carvings are the relief-carved *kakame* ("KAH-kah-meh") figures, traditionally connected with headhunting for ritual purposes and historically kept along with the racks of head trophies in the men's house.

The Sepik River is often called the River of Art. Along the river many things used by the people daily are lavishly decorated. Canoes, for example, are carved with decorative prows representing animals or people. Spirit masks, shields, and other large carvings are everywhere, and even clay bowls and cooking pots are decorated. In the Trobriand Islands, carving produces ornate and useful walking sticks, stools, and small tables, sometimes inlaid with mother-of-pearl. Shell jewelry, particularly if made from the valuable black coral, is popular in the coastal towns. The art of carving is displayed in finely crafted bowls made from dark wood polished painstakingly with a pig's tusk. The rims of some are patterned with the coastal themes of fish and turtle.

While some masks are custom-made for ceremonies, they are largely produced as ornaments.

WEAPONS, SHIELDS, AND MASKS

The creation of decorative weapons, shields, and masks throughout Papua New Guinea demonstrates the fundamental link between art and daily living. Weapons and shields have long been decorated for ceremonial occasions, and they help create the fearsome look of a warrior in full regalia. Stone axes in the Mt. Hagen region are worn across the back and are of ceremonial value only. Their slate blades are attached to the wooden handles with decorative woven cane strips. Some stone axes are etched with geometric motifs.

Sharp bone daggers, including the valued cassowary bone, are worn as an item of ornamentation, and the Hulis make small picks tipped with the slicing claws of cassowaries. Spears are bedecked with a variety of textile bindings, feathers, and shells, as well as with incised designs. Shields are endowed with a spiritual symbolism that is just as important as the physical task of defense. They are highly valued by collectors, as special care is taken when carving and decorating them.

The masks of Papua New Guinea show great diversity in styles and materials ranging from wood to turtleshell, and from 12 inches (30 cm) in length to a lofty 47 inches (119 cm). Masks from some areas look almost African, but the Sepik spirit masks are as distinctive as the rest of the carvings that come from that region. They are initially carved from wood, then covered in molded clay that has been embedded with teeth (mostly from pigs), hair, and shells. Some masks are used exclusively by male secret societies and may be woven from pith.

MALANGGAN MASKS

The wooden *malanggan* ("mah-LANG-gan") masks of New Ireland are some of the larger and more ornate masks. They are carved with elaborate panels depicting totemic animals and human figures in memory of the dead. *Malanggan* also refers to feasts and celebrations held at the end of the mourning period when the carvings are made. Traditionally only one man in the tribe is permitted to make or display these masks, and it is a highly coveted and respected role. A *malanggan* feast is an important occasion during which traditional teachings are passed on, but because of Christian conversions and the social effects of cash cropping, is now practiced only around the Tabar Islands, and less on New Ireland.

COLORFUL BILUMS

Bilums are the colorful woven net bags seen nearly everywhere in Papua New Guinea. They are traditionally made from natural materials such as rattan, dried leaves, grasses, and strong pandanus fiber. Modern materials such as plastic and nylon are increasingly being used, with an even more colorful result. The bags are strong and versatile, used to carry anything from a baby to huge loads of firewood. The process of making them is time-consuming, and most of the weaving is done by the women.

The weaving skills traditionally seen in basketry have been adapted in the highlands to create modern woolen blankets, bags, and bedspreads.

The bilum can be stretched to carry enormous loads supported by the head, leaving the hands free to perform other tasks.

LEISURE

IN A COUNTRY WHERE PEOPLE WORK LONG DAYS just to feed and clothe themselves, time for leisure is limited. When women are not busy gathering or preparing food, or collecting water and firewood, they occupy themselves by making handicrafts. Recreation therefore takes place largely at the end of the day with family members talking, listening to stories, or relaxing around the fire before turning in to bed. The work of the men tends to be hard but more sporadic, and they often have more time during the day which they spend congregating in the men's house, talking, or just smoking tobacco or chewing betel nut.

Papuan nationals have their famous *singsings* ("SING-sings") to provide a welcome break from the routine of daily chores. A *singsing* is any large celebration that incorporates feasting, drumming, dancing, and, as the name suggests, much singing. These are celebrated all over the country and can last for days.

Left: **Men escape the hustle and bustle of town to relax by a lake.**

Opposite: **A wheel and stick provide much fun for this child.**

BETEL NUT CHEWING

Betel nut or *buai* is the green nutlike fruit of the areca palm that is chewed for its mildly narcotic and stimulant effect. This effect is increased with the addition of a lime powder that acts as a catalyst, and people also chew the betel nut with sprigs of a bitter pepper plant to improve the flavor. The chemical reaction between the *buai* and the lime produces a bright red liquid accompanied by copious saliva. Indiscriminate spitting means that the red liquid often ends up on the pavements around town. The longterm chewing of betel nut causes the mouth to be dyed a bright red, while the teeth are permanently blackened. Occasionally such a practice leads to mouth cancer.

There are beliefs and customs that surround the betel nut. Some argue that without the lime, chewing the fibrous *buai* is a good teeth cleaner and mouth freshener in areas where toothbrushes are not used. Because of the copious salivation, it is said that chewing *buai* allows a person to work long hours in the sun without drinking water. Sometimes betel nut will be offered and shared

Those who chew betel nuts are easily recognized by their bright red lips and mouth.

between two parties once a dispute has been settled, as a token of peace.

There are sacred uses to the plant as well. It is believed that the chewing of *buai* with ginger or some other herb can help a man chase evil spirits away; as he spits he must recite magical words. A woman who wishes to bear a son will chew *buai* along with other herbs. At *singsings*, the dancers will chew betel nut so that they can stay awake and continue dancing for many hours. It is believed that sorcerers can use the leftovers of a chewed

betel nut to invoke magical spells that can cause death to the chewer. This produces in its believers a degree of care in disposing of their *buai* waste. In 1980 the Public Service Commission passed a ruling forbidding public servants from chewing betel nut at work, or any time that they are in a government building.

People chew on a little of the betel nut's green flesh with some lime powder that takes away the nut's sour taste.

URBAN PURSUITS

Urban centers offer a wider range of activities than restaurants and private clubs, which are frequented only by expatriates and those with cash. Small social gatherings among family and friends, with a meal included, are sometimes held at urban centers. This reflects the rural custom of gathering around the fire. Radio and television provide both entertainment and information for those with access to them, and movies are screened publicly in some towns.

Market days in the town and villages are opportunities to trade, shop, and talk with friends. Hotels and discotheques provide night entertainment in the larger towns, although their numbers are limited. In the towns there are clubs for all sorts of outdoor activities including team sports, bushwalking, sportfishing, boating, and diving.

SPORTS

The concept of team sports did not exist in Papua New Guinea before its colonization by the Europeans. Competitions in traditional skills—such as canoe races and displays of prowess in hunting, fishing, or other skills—were conducted by many groups, often associated with a *singsing* or feast. The Christian missionaries introduced many team sports that required a minimum of sports equipment, and they were much enjoyed and rapidly became popular. As a result most of the sports played in Papua New Guinea have a foreign origin, although athletics, boating, swimming, and skindiving are not far removed from traditional activities.

Football refers to three separate games of which rugby is the most popular. The play is rough, but no one seems to mind. Large games can turn into a sort of tribal warfare on the field when opposing groups play

Contact sports are quite dangerous for people who have suffered chronic malaria, as there is the risk of rupturing their enlarged spleens. However, this does nothing to dim the enthusiasm of Papuans who play football.

Baseball is one of many outdoor sports played in Papua New Guinea.

A softball team takes a
break in the noonday
heat.

against one another and sometimes give vent to underlying feelings of hostility. The spectators, who are passionate about supporting their favorite team, may join in and violence can erupt. Before long the riot squad makes its appearance, using tear gas to disperse the rowdy crowd. Rugby is played at the international, national, and local levels. Australian Rules Football, known as "Aussie rules," also has its adherents in the country, as does soccer.

Basketball, netball, softball, volleyball, and baseball are popular throughout the country, and these are sports in which women are more likely to participate. Other Western sports such as tennis, cricket, bicycle racing, and rock climbing are also enjoyed. As a member of the Commonwealth, Papua New Guinea can enter teams into the Commonwealth Games conducted every four years, as well as international sports events in Asia and the South Pacific. Boxer Tumak Sogolik was the first sportsperson to win a medal for Papua New Guinea in the Commonwealth Games held in Edmonton, Canada, in 1978.

SINGSINGS

Singsings are the national celebratory medium in Papua New Guinea, taking place on all sorts of occasions: seasonal feasts, paying a bride price, initiation rites, traditional exchange ceremonies, or even celebrating the win of a favored politician. It is a chance for the people to don their traditional finery and paint their bodies elaborately. Some of the feathers, magnificent headdresses, and shell jewelry worn are borrowed; new ones may also be made for the special occasion.

The dances almost always retell a traditional story or theme. Sometimes they are very heavily influenced by ritual; at other times they can be more spontaneous. Preparation for the dancers can include fasting or restricting themselves to traditional foods, staying inside the village enclosure, and speaking only with initiated men. Some parts of the *singsing* may have a more sacred significance, and women may be required to leave at that point. Some *singsings* may be accompanied by feasting and the exchange of gifts.

ASARO MUDMEN AND HIGHLAND SHOWS

One famous legend enacted in Asaro *singsings* revolves around the mudmen. It is said that warriors of the Mut tribe were driven back by their enemies into the nearby river. They emerged later, ghostly pale due to their covering of dried mud. Their enemies mistook them for evil spirits and fled in terror. This legend is relived by the dancers, who cover their bodies in the gray mud that, as it dries and flakes, represents the decaying flesh of the dead. Large rounded mud masks complete the illusion.

Highland shows, a variant of the *singsing*, are popular with residents and tourists. They are held in Mt. Hagen and Goroka around August or September of alternate years. The shows were designed to demonstrate the similarities and positive qualities of the various highland groups, and to foster goodwill towards strangers instead of suspicion and hostility.

In the early days of the highland shows, which started in the 1950s, as many as 40,000 warriors in full regalia would congregate and dance with their paints, feathers, and weapons flashing in the sun.

Mudmen from the village of Asaro, located in the Eastern Highlands province.

FESTIVALS

PAPUA NEW GUINEA'S MOST WIDELY CELEBRATED FESTIVAL is Independence Day, September 16. On that day celebrations and shows are staged throughout the country.

Seasonal festivals are held in various regions, such as the Yam Festival in the Trobriand Islands (June–July) and the Frangipani Festival in Rabaul on July 23 to commemorate the first flowers blooming after the 1937 eruption of the Matupit volcano in Rabaul. The *Hiri Moale* ("HEE-ree MOH-ah-le") Festival, held around Independence Day in Port Moresby, honors the ancient *hiri* trading voyages.

In addition to these regional festivities, smaller groups such as villages and tribes hold their own festivals. Some of these are seasonal spiritual observances; others, like the Engan *Tee* ("TEE") and highland *Moga* ("MOH-gah"), are special occasions where objects of wealth are ceremonially exchanged with neighboring or even enemy groups.

Left: **The tapioca dance performed by the men of the Trobriand Islands.**

Opposite: **Papua New Guinea's festivals call for large gatherings, colorful *singsings*, feasts, and parades. They are occasions in which people abandon their Western clothes to don traditional finery.**

Dancers at the *Hiri Moale*, a festival to commemorate the annual trading voyages of their ancestors.

INDEPENDENCE DAY AND HIRI MOALE

Papuan nationals celebrate the birth of their independence as a nation on September 16. While various ceremonies and shows are held all over the country, the biggest and most famous is the *Hiri Moale*, commemorating the ancient trading voyages made between villages in the Port Moresby area and the Gulf province.

Long before the arrival of Europeans, *hiri* trading voyages were conducted amid ritual procedures. The Motu people in the Port Moresby area made clay cooking pots that they traded for sago in the Gulf villages where sago was abundant. The voyages were necessary because the dry climate of the Port Moresby area did not favor farming, and the sago helped overcome the food shortage for the Motu. Cordial relations with the Gulf people also allowed many Motu young men to find brides without intermarrying among their own closely related people.

The building of the *hiri* canoes, called *lakatoi* ("LAH-kah-toy-e"), was supervised by two men who were honored to be selected for the role.

During the building of the canoes, they had to observe strict taboos by eating special foods, not communicating with their wives in any way, and not washing or cutting their hair.

The canoes for the voyages needed to be large and sturdy because hundreds of miles had to be covered by all the able-bodied men in the village. The bare shell of each boat was blessed early in its construction by a shaman, using a specially concocted incense smoke. Village women plaited together strips of palm fronds for the sails; these were then sewn together by the men. The sailors would depart in September when the seas were calm and the winds favorable. The villagers knew it would take at least 50 days before the winds changed to the northeast. A watch would be set up for the returning boats, and as the village waited in anticipation for their safe return, the people made preparations for a special feast.

The last *hiri* voyages occurred in the 1940s, but they are still honored. The festival provides an opportunity for the people to gather as in former days and celebrate with canoe races, *singsings*, processions, competitions among string-based bands, and other contests.

Motuan men were good sailors and had impressive boats with distinctive sails shaped like crabs' claws.

PUBLIC HOLIDAYS IN PAPUA NEW GUINEA

New Year's Day: January 1	Independence Day: September 16
Good Friday and Easter (variable)	Christmas Day: December 25
Queen's Birthday: mid-June	Boxing Day: December 26
Remembrance Day: July 23	

In addition, each province has its own provincial government holiday. These are usually observed on a Friday or a Monday to give workers a long holiday weekend.

Pig feasts are always a ceremonial affair and prepared according to custom. The pigs are killed with a bow and arrow, and their carcasses are placed over an open flame, after which they are removed and cut up. Clotted blood is sometimes collected in a gourd to be used later for magical purposes.

THE KULA RING

Another series of trading ceremonies involves a circle of islands in and around the Milne Bay province, including the Trobriand Islands. The early sea voyages by canoes are reenacted, although the distances covered today are not as long as before. Modern vessels are sometimes used, but elaborately decorated canoes are still favored.

The exchange of goods serves the purpose of spreading goodwill among the islanders. The items exchanged are decoratively carved armbands and special necklaces called *bagi* ("BAH-ghee"), made with red shells that are painstakingly ground by women into evenly proportioned circular disks. The exchanges are purely ritualistic and the goods rarely leave the trading ring, being "traded" between islands in the circuit. What is more significant is that the travelers are offered hospitality by their exchange partners. The armbands travel counterclockwise around the ring of islands, and the necklaces clockwise. The goods are passed through a complete circle in about five years. Besides the exchange of the ritual jewelry, it is also an important opportunity to trade in other goods, baskets, food, or pottery.

FRANGIPANI FESTIVAL

The Frangipani Festival is held in Rabaul, the capital of the East New Britain province, toward the end of July. This small-town event, which includes fireworks and a parade among its festivities, celebrates the blooming of the area's many frangipanis, the first flowers to reappear after the 1937 eruption of the Matupit volcano, located at the edge of the town. In commemoration of the event a small airplane flies overhead and drops hundreds of flowers over the parade.

EXCHANGE CEREMONIES: TEE AND MOGA

In some areas of Papua New Guinea, preparations for huge exchanges require several years between ceremonies; one reason is to collect the appropriate number of pigs. They are sometimes held to exchange "payback goods," but more often they are designed to display the big man's or clan's wealth.

One ceremony is held specifically to repay debts incurred, and extra items are added to the repayment. In the highlands the ceremonies are called *Moga*, while the Engans (from Enga province in the highlands) have a similar custom called the *Tee*. These ceremonies are accompanied by all the trimmings of a *singsing*. Goods exchanged include pigs, kina shells, and even cartons of beer. Many of the pigs are slaughtered, and the feasting can continue for several days. The repetition of these exchanges means that at some point in time, the giver will get back things similar to whatever he has given or more. The larger exchanges can include not only gift-giving and dancing, but marriages and initiation ceremonies as well.

The chief's yam house is always the first to be filled after a harvest.

TROBRIAND YAM HARVESTING

In the Trobriand Islands, the taro yams cultivated for food are of greater importance than mere nourishment; people take pride in the size and quality of the yams they grow. The yams are a sort of status symbol and an indicator of farming skills. The men sometimes spend hours discussing the cultivation of yams and it is an honor to be known as a good yam grower.

Yam harvesting takes place around July or August each year. As they are dug up, yams are displayed and admired by all in the gardens. The women flank the procession in which the yams are carried back to the village by the men; the yams are then displayed in circular piles and admired again.

The village is arranged around the central yam houses. These form an inner ring that is surrounded by the sleeping houses, and these in turn are surrounded by trees. The yam houses are used for storage but are open enough to display the number of yams inside.

A man has one yam house for each of his wives, and it is the responsibility of his wife's clan to fill that yam house, while the owner fills someone else's. Again there are rituals to be observed, and the chief's yam house is always the first to be filled. In this way the yams form part of the ceremonial exchange that cements the ongoing relationship and goodwill among the island's villages.

The yam harvest and its accompanying celebrations can last up to three months. It is a time of much feasting, dancing, singing, and general festivities.

MAPRIK YAM FESTIVALS

The celebration of the yam harvest is observed differently in the Maprik region near the Sepik area. Yams are the staple food there, grown on distinctive trellises. In some instances their cultivation and harvest are the work of the men, carried out in secret away from the women. The yams are stored in special huts, but for the harvest festival the largest yams are collected amid much ritual and singing, and decorated with woven masks, or painted with faces so they look like human figures.

In a good year, some of the yams will reach a spectacular 10 feet (3 meters) in length, although usually the largest ones would be about 6 to 7 feet (1.8–2.1 meters) long. After the harvest has been praised and the celebrations accomplished, the displayed yams are presented to the women as gifts.

Men rejoicing in a village clearing after a successful yam harvest. The tall structures in the background are yam storage houses.

FOOD

UNLIKE MANY OTHER COUNTRIES, Papua New Guinea does not have a distinctive cuisine. There are no special ingredients or flavors to capture the attention of cooks around the world. Many people prepare food at the subsistence level, eating bland and unchanging diets based on sweet potatoes or sago for breakfast, lunch, and dinner.

No spices are used, although ginger is added to the cooking in some areas; it may also be put into freshly brewed black tea for drinking. Salt is used heavily throughout the country; it is added to the food for flavor, or used as a preservative when fresh meat is available.

Most people's diets are deficient in protein. Whenever possible, protein is obtained by fishing in rivers and in coastal areas, the rearing of chickens for food, and the hunting of small marsupials. Where taboos do not exist, some game birds are also hunted. Along the Sepik, crocodile flesh is an occasional addition.

Left: **Yam and sweet potatoes feature prominently in the people's diet.**

Opposite: **Food being prepared over an open stove.**

Cooking a meal of sea cucumbers.

The nation imports large quantities of canned fish and rice; mixed together, they are a staple dish for the people. Sometimes all that is available in a trade store are canned fish, rice, salt, and tobacco. Pigs are kept for status and not for their food value, and are slaughtered only on special occasions, when they provide much appreciated meat. Papuans grow a wide variety of tropical fruit and vegetables, and some have even planted Western vegetables in their gardens.

Kitchens in the urban centers are set up in the Western style, with electric stoves, metal pots and pans, running water, storage cupboards, dishes, and silverware. In the rural areas, cooking is carried out over wood fires, either inside or outside the house; sometimes there is a special open-sided *haus-wind* ("HOWS-wind") hut where the cooking fire is located. Unglazed clay pots are used in the cooking, while large feasts are prepared in ground ovens. Food is eaten from rough baskets, banana leaves, or coconut shell halves. Metal pans are increasingly common where once only clay pots were available.

For large feasts, a clay ground oven called a *mumu* ("MOO-moo") is used. This is essentially a hole in the earth lined with stones that have been heated for several hours by a well-fed fire. The size of the pit depends on the number of people being catered for, whether it is a few dozen or several hundred. A pig is the essential ingredient, along with yams or sweet potatoes; other ingredients that are available may also be included. Cooking in a *mumu* is a slow process, and the people sing, dance, and tell stories while waiting for the food to cook. When ready, the cooked food is served in order of seniority, on banana leaves.

The simplest and yet paradoxically most lavish cooking style in Papua New Guinea is that using the ground oven. For feasts, the pit may be several hundred feet long and it is filled with hundreds of whole pigs.

A GROUND-OVEN FEAST

Fresh banana leaves (kitchen foil is a substitute)
Fleshy young pandanus fruit (or small onions, peeled and left whole)
Yams and sweet potatoes, chopped into sizable pieces
Vegetables in season; pumpkin is optional
Pork, cut into large chunks
Green leafy vegetables

This makes a wonderful barbeque, but you will need adults to help you prepare the pit and hot stones. Leave out the vegetables you cannot find.

Choose a dry area and dig a hole; use coals to create a hot pit. Line the bottom and sides with banana leaves and scatter handfuls of pandanus fruit or onions. Add a layer of yams or sweet potatoes, and another layer of vegetables in season or pumpkin. Add pork, along with green leafy vegetables that will simmer in the meat juice. Cover the food with a layer of banana leaves and roll live coal over the top of the leaves—be careful not to burn yourself. Seal the oven with earth. After about two hours, uncover the earth, pull the coal aside, and share the food. The amount of ingredients used and the cooking time vary according to the number of people being served.

Above: **It takes great skill to skin a crocodile so that the hide comes off in one piece. The hide is sold while the flesh can be eaten.**

Opposite: **Fish on sale at a market.**

HUNTING AND FISHING

Hunting is an activity enjoyed by the men; it also provides a valuable addition to the diet, particularly in areas where the staple is sago, a crop that is abundant but not high in vitamins. Shotguns and rifles are increasingly common throughout the country, and are more lethal than the traditional hunting weapons of spears and bows and arrows. Wild pigs, wild dogs, bandicoots, tree possums, wallabies, and birds are targets for the hunters. Great skill is often required to find and kill these animals as they are often quite small.

It takes a skilled person to hunt crocodiles because they are powerful and potentially dangerous. At night, a hunter shines a flashlight in a crocodile's glowing eyes, dazzling it and allowing a canoe to get close enough for the hunter to kill it with a long harpoon, aided by the blow of an ax to a softer part of the armored creature's body. During the day and in shallow water, pairs of skilled hunters search around slowly with their feet in the clay of the river bed until they find the scaly hide of the smaller New Guinea crocodile. One hunter will duck underwater and pull the surprised and thrashing creature up, while the other uses a large, well-aimed knife to kill it. Crocodile skin is quite valuable, and the meat from a large crocodile can be enough to feed a whole village.

Fishing is carried out by ingenious methods. A large variety of fish and shellfish are caught and eaten, including crayfish, prawns, and crabs. Spears and bows and arrows are popular, while some fishers use nets or fishing lines. Huge basketlike fish traps are woven in some areas, standing taller than the fishermen. Smaller traps made of thorny materials are woven into a cone shape and baited. Fish attempting to feed on the bait are caught on the thorns.

In other areas, a mild poison called rotenone, which paralyzes the respiratory system, is made by crushing a vine root. The poison is poured into the water, and the fishers simply wait for the fish to float to the surface. In New Ireland, some men attract sharks to their canoes, either with their voices or with a rattle made from coconut shells. A noose attached to a piece of wood is slipped around the shark's body. Dragging this device slows the shark and tires it. Once the animal has tired it is speared or bludgeoned, but even then it usually puts up a fight while being hauled into the canoe.

Both fish and other animal meats are eaten freshly cooked where possible and any surplus is salted and dried, or sometimes smoked over a slow fire. Cooking methods include utilizing the slowbaking ground ovens, roasting over glowing coals, or boiling in a clay pot with water, sweet potatoes, and greens.

BREEDING CROCODILES

Overhunting has greatly reduced the number of crocodiles along the Sepik, and farming them is a profitable alternative. Instead of capturing the grown crocodiles for farming, they are left in the wild and the younger crocodiles and eggs are collected instead. As the eggs are often laid on floating clumps of vegetation and guarded ferociously by their territorial mothers, modern methods are used to gather them. A helicopter lowers a nimble individual on a rope who hastily collects several of the eggs before the mother has a chance to attack. The local landowners are paid for each egg collected on their land, providing a valuable source of income.

Women processing the sago palm to extract its starchy flour.

SAGO AS A STAPLE FOOD

Sago, or *saksak* ("SACK-sack") as it is called in Pidgin, is the starchy food eaten by all the groups of people who live in the swampy areas of the country, especially along the Sepik and its tributaries. It is very bland and nearly pure starch, and while it provides energy, it lacks the vitamins and minerals that other plant foods usually provide. Sago is important because it grows in areas where it is nearly impossible to cultivate other crops because of frequent flooding and waterlogged soils.

The process of obtaining sago is a lengthy one. The sago palm grows for about 15 years, storing starch inside its trunk before it flowers—which it does only once in its life. It must be harvested at that point, or the starch is converted into a massive spike of flowers, after which the palm dies. In the past, a ceremony was conducted before chopping the palm down to appease the ancestor spirit believed to reside in every sago palm, but this is rarely done now.

The tree is cut down by men, and dragged or floated closer to the village or to a convenient clearing where the bark is stripped. The pith inside is chopped and pulped, again by men. Then the women's job begins. They beat and wash the pith repeatedly with water to extract the starch, and the water is collected. The starch forms a thick, gluey mass at the bottom. It is dried to form a flour which stores well and is the basis of sago consumption.

There are three basic ways to prepare sago. It can be cooked immediately before it has dried into flour, or else the flour is boiled in water into a thick glutinous porridge to which is added fish, coconut, or some vegetables. The second method is to mix it with a little water to form a thick pancake that is fried on both sides in a very hot pan without fat or oil. The third is to simply pour the sago into the hot pan. The sago hardens immediately, and it is flattened and turned to cook on the other side. The resultant pancakes are known as *parem* ("PAH-rem"), and tend to be crispy on the outside and soft and chewy on the inside. These flat cakes are convenient too; people can carry them on their daily tasks and eat them when needed.

Sago starch can be cooked in many ways.

MANY USES OF THE SAGO

Neil Nightingale, writing in *New Guinea, An Island Apart* (BBC Books, 1992), states that the sago palm is used for more than just food. Its leaves are used as roofing material, and its young shoots are split and the fibers made into grass skirts, or spun into long lengths of string. Sago thorns come in handy as needles, while the outside of the leaf stems are woven into fish traps. The bark is split, flattened, and made into floorboards, fashioned into storage jars, or burnt to extract its salt content.

Above: **Sweet potato needs minimal preparation and can be eaten on its own.**

Opposite: **Woman husking a coconut; its flesh can be eaten and the water contained in its hollow makes a refreshing drink.**

SWEET POTATOES, YAMS, AND OTHER VEGETABLES

There are many varieties of sweet potatoes, differing in color, texture, size, and flavor; these are the staple carbohydrate source in many areas, particularly in the highlands. Sweet potatoes are quite nutritious but do not form a balanced diet in themselves. Known as *kaukau* ("KOW-kow") in Pidgin, they can be roasted whole, cut up and boiled with meat and other vegetables, steamed with other food in banana leaves, or baked in a *mumu*.

While men may be involved in the initial preparation of the garden, and even the planting of the *kaukau* and yams, it is the women who tend the gardens. The men prepare the fields for planting by cutting tree roots left in the field and digging the soil to loosen it. The women's work involves breaking up large pieces of earth and preparing mounds of the earth for planting. They then push pieces of *kaukau* or yam vine into the mounds, leaving a small part exposed. While waiting for the vines to grow the women have to attend to the weeding. In three or four months, new vines will spread and cover the ground; under the soil are new *kaukau* or yams to be harvested.

People tend to harvest only a few sweet potatoes at a time because the damp climate causes food in storage to rot readily. The importance of *kaukau* in the diet is reflected in the arrangement of the garden: other crops are never accorded more than a quarter of the cultivated land.

Some groups of sweet potato growers in the highlands have an efficient way to grow their crops despite the cooler temperatures. They build large

120

low mounds of soil over old vegetation, and these form the planting beds for the sweet potatoes. As the old vegetation decomposes, the compost adds vital nutrients to the soil besides raising the temperature of the mounds, thus protecting the plants on cold nights.

In a Papua New Guinea garden, you might find any of the following: three or four varieties of sweet potatoes, yams, small starchy bananas for cooking, peanuts, long green beans, local leafy green vegetables, maize, chili, cassava (whose roots yield the starchy tapioca), sugarcane, ginger, pumpkin, pitpit cane (the flower is edible), pandanus, breadfruit, papaya, and even tobacco. There are often coconut palms nearby.

Many of these vegetables and fruit are cooked by the same methods as for the sweet potato, but the coconut is widely included in other mixes of food. Fresh green coconut is moist and creamy in flavor, unlike the desiccated variety found on supermarket shelves. It is commonly grated into a fine mash and added directly to the pot, or else the grated coconut is wrapped in a piece of coarse cloth that is squeezed tightly to extract the coconut milk from it. When coconut milk is added to the meal, especially to cooked rice, the food is rich in flavor and delicious.

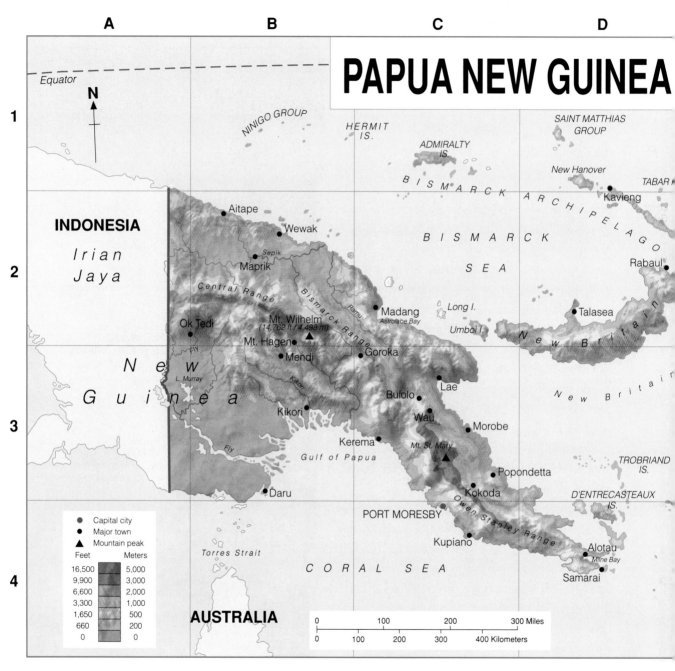

PAPUA NEW GUINEA

A · B · C · D

1 · 2 · 3 · 4

Equator

N

NINIGO GROUP

HERMIT IS.

ADMIRALTY IS.

SAINT MATTHIAS GROUP

New Hanover

TABAR I

Kavieng

BISMARCK

ARCHIPELAGO

INDONESIA

Irian Jaya

Aitape

Wewak

Sepik

Maprik

Central Range

Ok Tedi

Mt. Wilhelm
(14,762 ft / 4,498 m)

Mt. Hagen

Mendi

Bismarck Range

Ramu

Madang

Astrolabe Bay

Goroka

BISMARCK

SEA

Long I.

Umboi I.

Rabaul

Talasea

New Britain

N e w   B r i t a i n

N e w

G u i n e a

L. Murray

Fly

Kikori

Kikori

Bulolo

Wau

Lae

Morobe

Kerema

Mt. St. Mary

Gulf of Papua

Fly

Daru

Popondetta

Kokoda

TROBRIAND IS.

D'ENTRECASTEAUX IS.

PORT MORESBY

Owen Stanley Range

Kupiano

Alotau

Milne Bay

Samarai

Capital city
Major town
Mountain peak

Feet	Meters
16,500	5,000
9,900	3,000
6,600	2,000
3,300	1,000
1,650	500
660	200
0	0

Torres Strait

C O R A L   S E A

AUSTRALIA

0 · 100 · 200 · 300 Miles
0 · 100 · 200 · 300 · 400 Kilometers

E **F**

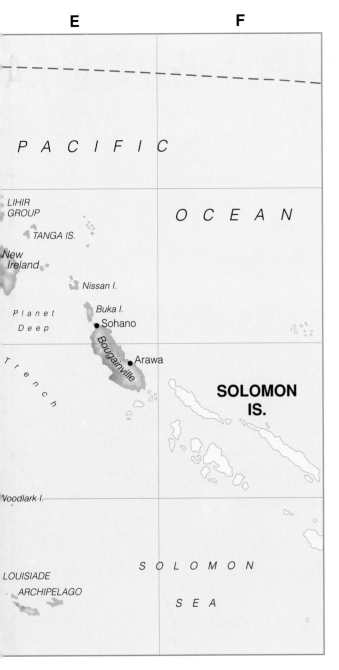

P A C I F I C

O C E A N

LIHIR
GROUP

TANGA IS.

New
Ireland

Nissan I.

Planet
Deep

Buka I.
Sohano

Bougainville

Arawa

T r e n c h

**SOLOMON
IS.**

Woodlark I.

S O L O M O N

LOUISIADE
ARCHIPELAGO

S E A

New Britain, D2
New Britain Trench,
  D3-E3
New Guinea, A3-B3
New Hanover, D1
New Ireland, E2
Ninigo Group, B1
Nissan Island, E2

Ok Tedi, B2
Owen Stanley Range,
  C3-D4

Pacific Ocean, E1
Planet Deep, E2
Popondetta, C3
Port Moresby, C4

Rabaul, D2
Ramu River, B2-C2

Saint Matthias Group, D1
Samarai, D4
Sepik River, B2
Sohano, E2
Solomon Islands, F3
Solomon Sea, F4
St. Mary, Mt., C3

Tabar Islands, D1
Talasea, D2
Tanga Island, E2
Torres Strait, B4
Trobriand Islands, D3

Umboi Island, C2

Wau, C3
Wewak, B2
Wilhelm, Mt., B2
Woodlark Island, E3

ikori River, B3
okoda, C3
upiano, C4

ae, C3
ihir Group, E2
ong Island, C2
ouisiade Archipelago, E4

Madang, C2
Maprik, B2
Mendi, B3
Milne Bay, D4
Morobe, C3
Mt. Hagen , B2
Murray, Lake, B3

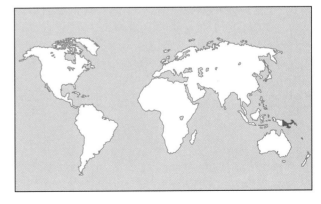

QUICK NOTES

LAND AREA
178,656 square miles (462,840 square km)

POPULATION
4.4 million

CAPITAL
Port Moresby

REGIONAL CENTERS
Lae, Madang, Wewak, and Goroka

PROVINCES
National Capital District (Port Moresby) and 19 provinces: Central, Oro, Milne Bay, Morobe, Madang, Manus, North Solomons, East Sepik, Western, Sandaun, Gulf, Eastern Highlands, Western Highlands, Southern Highlands, Simbu, Enga, East New Britain, West New Britain, and New Ireland

NATIONAL SYMBOL
Bird of Paradise (*Genus Paradisaea*) perched on a *kundu* ceremonial drum, a barbed spear behind the drum.

NATIONAL FLAG
Diagonally divided from the top of the hoist to the bottom of the fly. A yellow bird of paradise is centered on the upper red triangle; the lower triangle is black with the white Southern Cross constellation centered.

MAJOR RIVERS
Sepik and Fly rivers, navigable by small boats for around 500 miles (800 km).

HIGHEST POINT
Mt. Wilhelm 14,762 feet (4,498 meters) above sea level

NATIONAL ANIMAL
Bird of paradise

NATIONAL/OFFICIAL LANGUAGES
English is the official language, but Pidgin and Motu are widely spoken.

MAJOR RELIGION
Christianity

CURRENCY
1 kina = 100 toea ("TOH-yah")
(US$1 = 138 toea)

MAIN EXPORTS
Copper, gold, coffee, palm oil, cocoa, timber logs, prawns, and fish.

IMPORTANT DATE
Independence Day, September 16

IMPORTANT POLITICIANS
Michael T. Somare, Sir Julius Chan, Paias Wingti, Rabbie Namaliu, and Bill Skate

GLOSSARY

bilum ("BILL-uhm")
Strong woven string bag made and carried by the women.

buai ("BWAI")
Betel nut.

guvmen ("GUV-men")
Government.

handet ("HAN-dett")
Hundred.

haus tamborans ("house TAM-bor-ans")
Spirit houses storing items of cultural and religious significance.

hiri ("hih-REE")
Ancient trading expedition.

kaikai ("KHAI-khai")
Food.

kaukau ("KOW-kow")
Sweet potato.

kundu ("KUHN-doo")
Drum featured on Papua New Guinea's coat of arms.

kwik piksa leta ("KWIK PIK-sa LET-tah")
Quick picture letter, that is, a faxed letter.

laplap ("LAP-lap")
Loincloth or a piece of cloth.

luluai ("loo-loo-AY")
Headman.

masalai ("mass-ah-LAY")
Crocodile.

Motu
Language originally used by the Motuan people in the Port Moresby region, now more widely spoken.

mumu ("MOO-moo")
Oven dug into the ground.

naiswan ("NAIS-wan")
Expression of congratulations or approval, derived from the English words "nice one."

parem ("PAH-rem")
A sago pancake.

singsing ("SING-sing")
Any large celebration with feasting, music, and dancing.

taul ("TAH-ol")
Towel.

tausen ("TAU-ssen")
Thousand.

Tok Pisin ("TOHK pee-sin")
The Pidgin language.

wantok ("WAN-tohk")
System of reciprocity that emphasizes sharing and mutual help between families, clans, or tribes; derived from the English phrase "one talk."

BIBLIOGRAPHY

Dodwell, Christina. *In Papua New Guinea.* Somerset: Oxford Illustrated Press, 1983.

Dorney, Sean. *Papua New Guinea—People, Politics and History Since 1975.* Sydney: Random House Australia, 1990.

Fox, Mary. *Enchantment of the World: Papua New Guinea.* Chicago: Children's Press, 1994.

Nightingale, Neil. *New Guinea, An Island Apart.* London: BBC Books, 1992.

Office of Information. *This is Papua New Guinea.* Papua New Guinea Government, 1980.

Turner, Mark. *Papua New Guinea: The Challenge of Independence.* Penguin Books Australia, 1990.

Waiko, John Dademo. *A Short History of Papua New Guinea.* Melbourne: Oxford University Press, 1993.

Wheeler, Tony and Murray, Jon. *Papua New Guinea, A Travel Survival Kit.* Melbourne: Lonely Planet Publications, 1993.

INDEX

INDEX

INDEX

PICTURE CREDITS